JIM CLARK

By DOUG NYE

PHOTOGRAPHS BY

DAVE FRIEDMAN

GRAHAM GAULD

GEOFF GODDARD

DAVID PHIPPS

NIGEL SNOWDON

OTHER TITLES IN THIS SERIES

Nigel Mansell
Niki Lauda
Alain Prost
Gilles Villeneuve
Emerson Fittipaldi
Jochen Rindt
Nelson Piquet

HAZLETON PUBLISHING

PUBLISHER
Richard Poulter

EXECUTIVE PUBLISHER
Elizabeth Le Breton

ART EDITOR
Steve Small

PRODUCTION MANAGER
George Greenfield

HOUSE EDITOR
Peter Lovering

PRODUCTION ASSISTANT
Deirdre Fenney

STATISTICS
John Taylor

Colour photography by:
David Phipps – front and back covers, pages 66 *(bottom)*,
73 *(top)*, 74, 77 and 80.

Geoff Goddard – pages 65, 66 *(top)*, 67, 68, 69, 70, 71, 72, 75,
76 and 78-9.

Dave Friedman – page 73 *(bottom)*.

Black and white photographs contributed by:
Dave Friedman, Graham Gauld, Geoff Goddard, David Phipps
and Nigel Snowdon.

This first edition published in 1991 by
Hazleton Publishing, 3 Richmond Hill, Richmond,
Surrey TW10 6RE.

ISBN: 0-905138-77-5

Printed in England by BAS Printers Ltd, Over Wallop,
Hampshire.

Typesetting by First impression Ltd, Richmond, Surrey.

ACKNOWLEDGEMENT

Within the space available we have tried to present an impression of Jim Clark the man, his formative influences and the truly revered personality he became. The quotes used are a selection from dozens of reminiscences collected from those who knew and who worked with Jimmy day-to-day, while his own words are extracts from *Jim Clark at the Wheel* (Arthur Barker, London, 1964), which was the fine, albeit arguably premature, autobiography ghosted by our friend Graham Gauld in celebration of Jim's first World Championship crown. For further reading we would also absolutely recommend *Jim Clark – Portrait of a Great Driver*, edited by Graham Gauld (Paul Hamlyn, Feltham, 1968 *et seq*), and *The Jim Clark Story* by Bill Gavin (Leslie Frewin, London, 1967).

DISTRIBUTORS

UK & OTHER MARKETS
George Philip Limited, 59 Grosvenor Street
London W1X 9DA

USA & CANADA
Motorbooks International, PO Box 2
729 Prospect Avenue, Osceola
Wisconsin 54020, USA

AUSTRALIA
Technical Book & Magazine Co. Pty
289-299 Swanston Street
Melbourne, Victoria 3000

Universal Motor Publications
c/o Automoto Motoring Bookshop
152-154 Clarence Street
Sydney 2000, New South Wales

NEW ZEALAND
David Bateman Limited, 'Golden Heights'
32-34 View Road, Glenfield, Auckland 10

PROLOGUE

Colin Chapman pored intently over photographs spilled chaotically across his desk at Ketteringham Hall. In his cavernous office there he had been, untypically, reminiscing about 'the old days' of Team Lotus. We had provided the photographs to prime his memory, hopefully to relax him, reining him down to the kind of intellectual speed which we mere mortals could match. He was always the most *electric* man I have ever known. Small wonder some of his lads nicknamed him 'The White Tornado'.

Over curling shots of long-obsolescent Lotuses, he had been patiently explaining all kinds of semi-technical detail. Now we knew why that particular slot had been cut there, why this folded angle had been riveted onto that surface, why – between those two races – one particular pick-up point had been moved...

As the hour which he had promised us stretched into two, then three, the crisp, clipped 'media' Colin Chapman – the hyper-dynamic millionaire tycoon – was submerged beneath the lifelong motor racing enthusiast within. We realised we were in good shape when he commanded, 'Stop all my calls...', and as the photographs sparked old memories so the anecdotes had begun to flow, and his old North London accent and phrasing had re-emerged. We laughed a lot that day. I would never claim to have known him at all well, but that afternoon was the closest we ever came.

Only one call came through, Sue his secretary leaning around the door and clearing her throat apologetically to explain, 'I thought you would like to take this one; Mr Ecclestone is on the line...' Colin gave us such an exaggerated wink it would have done credit to Fagin, and chuckled, 'Ooh, 'scuse me, it's me *Guv'nor*,' before taking the call.

Yes, he was that relaxed.

And then he had moved another print aside and beneath it was a shot of Jim Clark lying back in the cockpit of one of their Lotuses, head tilted to one side, gazing attentively up at the man who had created those winning cars for him, Chapman himself.

And our laughter subsided. It was over a decade since Jim had died behind the wheel of one such car. Colin gazed intently, silently, down at that picture, a half-smile on his handsome face. A question welled within me. I sensed this was not the time to ask it. That was not the kind of silence which anyone with an ounce of sensitivity would comfortably break.

After so much discussion, so much hilarity, it seemed interminable. In fact I doubt it lasted more than ten seconds, but by the dynamic Chapman's standards that was an age.

He was the one who broke the spell. He glanced up, caught my eye, and blinked as if startled awake from a brief day-dream. Never one to betray private emotion, he spoke instantly, crisply – but quietly – his right index finger tapping on the print. His simple, soft, words spoke volumes.

'*He* was the finest man I ever knew. As a driver he was a complete genius...

'And, do you know, I doubt if he ever fully realised it...'

Back in the days when two-thirds of the world atlas were coloured red as part of the Empire, the British schoolboy learned to expect an heroic set of characteristics from any sporting hero. Whether he read *Boy's Own Paper*, *Hotspur*, *Tiger* or *The Eagle*, the archetypal British sportsman was universally portrayed there as modest, magnanimous and unassuming in triumph; cheerful, philosophical and sporting in defeat. By instinct all reasonable schoolboys simply knew that the British sporting hero would conduct himself at all times with peerless honesty and integrity. He would be mild-mannered, gentlemanly, always approachable – generous with his time.

When fascination with motor racing submerged my boyhood love of cricket, I had been following 'Stirly' Moss since I was five, and then there was Mike Hawthorn from up the road in Farnham and look at all the nice things the journalists were writing about that Argentine, Fangio. Of course, he couldn't help being a foreigner – yet hadn't he won five World Championship titles with a grace and manner which matched our British sporting ideals?

Fangio retired in 1958 with 24 championship Grand Prix wins to his credit, a wonderful record, and a wonderful Man. That year saw Mike Hawthorn become the first British driver ever to win the drivers' world title, then he retired and within three months died in a stupid road accident. Stirling Moss was even then fully established as 'Mr Motor Racing'; absolutely Fangio's natural heir, the showman, businessman, master racing driver by whom all others measured their skill.

As the 1950s tapered away into the early 1960s, motor racing – even at its topmost levels – remained a relatively amateurish, informal, haphazard kind of sport. There was little uniformity to the manner in which even the great World Championship Grands Prix were run, and there was ample space in the calendar for a delicious rota of Formula 1 non-championship races in support.

At those minor meetings, mainly here in England, one could see the great Grand Prix drivers of the day plying their trade not only in their regular F1 cars for the feature event, but also in sports, GTs and touring cars too. It really was a terrific period of motor racing, and a hyper-active one for the finest drivers; all true Sport – and genuine Sportsmanship.

It was against this background – after Moss's career-ending crash at Goodwood at the start of 1962 – that Jim Clark emerged as his natural heir, the new standard-setter of his time, and the man who would eventually break Fangio's career record of Grand Prix victories. Jim's racing achievements are so familiar that even here, in this mini-biography, it seems almost superfluous to detail them.

During the 1960s he became a household name. Yet his was neither a regular face on TV, nor a familiar voice on radio. He avoided what would today be described as media hype. Self-projection was not for him. He simply let his driving do that projection for him. His God-given talent was such that he could out-race his peers in almost any kind of car – Formula 1, Formula 2, Indianapolis, any size or kind of sports or GT, and of course saloon cars too.

To anyone who saw him drive, his name is special. To almost all those fortunate enough to have known him, it is magical.

Now of course it's easy to idealise such a man and such a character, to view Clark the man with a rosy, nostalgic glow. But there's no need. Simply examine the objective facts, analyse one's own memories and plumb those of people who were close to him, and – warts and all – the reality is fine enough. Of course Jim Clark the man had his share of faults and failings. He was amazingly, almost terminally, indecisive outside the cockpit of a racing car. The fastidious might recoil from his constant chewing at his fingernails. Anyone expecting a hard-drinking, rugged, extrovert 'character' would have been disappointed. At the height of a lavish party opening the Spanish autodrome at Jarama in '67 I found him sitting cheerfully alone in a deep sofa, sipping a fruit juice, ready to converse with anyone willing to talk to him, not *vice versa*. He was also far too well mannered to gaze distractedly over the shoulder of any fan or autograph hunter who might have cornered him somewhere, looking for somebody more important to happen by. Such behaviour, common in superstars since Clark's day, would have been entirely foreign to him. Although by nature retiring, he remained a friendly and approachable person. He might seldom initiate some fun, a lark, but if others triggered one he would readily join in.

Above all he is recalled primarily as a natural and civilised gentleman who also happened to be an outstanding sportsman. Against our imbued ideal of the civilised British sporting hero, Jim Clark – the Border farmer turned World Champion racing driver – typified so many traditional values it hurts...

When he died, an era arguably died with him.

Perhaps one of his most impressive old-time virtues was simple loyalty. Uniquely among significant post-war racing drivers, Jim Clark spent his entire Formula 1 career driving for just one team. Right to the core, he was a Team Lotus man. Overall, including other classes in addition to Formula 1, from his first drive for Team in a Formula Junior car in 1960 to the time of his death in April 1968, Jimmy raced cars which did not bear a Lotus badge on only 19 occasions, and 15 of those involved Border Reivers and Essex Racing Stable team Aston Martin sports and GT cars within only the first three seasons of that span – 1960–1962.

But then, amazingly, through the following five and a bit seasons from 1963 to 1968, he competed in cars other than Lotuses or Lotus-Cortinas on only four occasions. The first of them was the very first serious saloon car race of his career, driving Alan Brown's huge 7-litre V8 Ford Galaxie at Brands Hatch on August Monday, 1963. Not until August Brands '66 did he again drive something other than a Lotus – Peter Westbury's fascinating BRM V8-engined four-wheel drive Felday sports-racing car. In October '67 at Rockingham Motor Speedway, Alabama, he drove a NASCAR Ford Fairlane stock car, and finally – the following month – in the Rex Mays 300 road race at Riverside, California, he raced Rolla Vollstedt's Ford V8-powered Indy car. Note that even in these four outings there's another marque loyalty, all but the Felday being Ford powered.

Such commitment to one marque, over such a lengthy period by such a significant racing driver, is unique.

Where Grand Prix racing alone is concerned it is unparalleled in post-war racing history, and for any near-equals one has to delve back pre-war to Manfred von Brauchitsch's commitment to Mercedes-Benz, and to Bernd Rosemeyer's tragically abbreviated career with Auto Union.

Jim Clark was very much Colin Chapman's driver, and friend, and it was a partnership which perhaps made them both great, joint authors of parallel legends...

Before examining his story, and the man, in detail, it's simple to summarise his career. After promising first steps in club racing he made his single-seater race debut on 26 December 1959 – a depressing one-off outing in a front-engined Formula Junior Gemini at a damp Boxing Day Brands Hatch meeting. That same day saw him suffer his first racing accident when he spun his friend Ian Scott-Watson's Lotus Elite.

Through friends and supporters he had won a test drive for the Aston Martin works team and earned a Formula 1 contract from Reg Parnell, their team manager. With that F1 ride supposedly signed up, Colin Chapman offered him a separate deal for Formula 2 and Formula Junior drives between Grands Prix, using the latest rear-engined works-entered Lotus 18s. When Aston's 1960 F1 programme collapsed, they released him to handle a third Team Lotus F1 entry. As the latest rear-engined Lotus set new performance standards in all three classes, so Jim's first Team Lotus season yielded nine wins.

By the time of the Dutch GP at Zandvoort in June, Colin Chapman was convinced of Jimmy's immense potential, and he made his World Championship F1 debut there, running as high as fourth before his car's gearbox failed. Two weeks later he finished fifth and scored his first World Championship points in the daunting Belgian GP at Spa

– despite witnessing the aftermath of two fatal accidents, to his team-mate Alan Stacey and to Cooper driver Chris Bristow.

By 1961 he was a permanent member of the Lotus F1 team. He was only 25 years old but had become the complete professional racing driver, totally absorbed in his work and loving almost every moment of it. He scored his first F1 wins that season, beginning on Easter Monday in the round-the-houses race at Pau, and following up with a hat-trick in the Springbok series of F1 races which closed the season – the Rand, Natal and South African GPs.

Tragedy again marred his season, for in the Italian GP at Monza his Lotus had collided with the Ferrari driven by Wolfgang von Trips, the popular German ace and 14 spectators being killed while Jimmy escaped unharmed.

His innate ability and enthusiasm kept him racing, and once snugged down into the body-hugging cockpit of his Lotuses his mind buried these darker moments and man and car became fused in a manner seldom seen before, or since.

For 1962 Colin Chapman introduced his monocoque Lotus 25 for Formula 1 and Jim won his first World Championship-qualifying Grand Prix in it, at Spa – the super-fast, dangerous and threatening circuit which he freely confessed he feared. Even so, he would win the next three Belgian GPs there on the trot…admittedly with luck on his side, but in the years he did not genuinely win the race on merit he was always running hard enough to benefit when the leaders struck trouble.

The 1962 World Championship season became a battle to the wire between Clark for Lotus and Graham Hill for BRM. Jimmy won the British and United States GPs, plus five minor non-championship F1 events, and he only lost his chance of championship victory in the deciding race in South Africa. He was actually leading comfortably when the omission of a star washer during assembly allowed a bolt to drop out of his Coventry-Climax V8 engine, its oil pumped away through the hole, and his challenge literally went up in smoke.

So Graham Hill won the championship that year, but in 1963 nobody could live with Jimmy and his Lotus 25s. He scored a record seven *Grande Épreuve* victories, four of them in succession, and at 27 became the youngest World Champion Driver yet.

That unique year also saw him make his American speedway debut in the classic Indianapolis 500, and he stunned the American USAC establishment there by all but winning in a tiny rear-engined Lotus-Ford which they had initially taken as a joke.

Jim still remained the modest, unassuming Border farmer despite all the glitz and glamour which now surrounded him. He was uncomfortable yet capable in the limelight, unassuming and friendly out of it – and greased lightning in a racing car.

He was an inquisitive driver – always keen to experience something new. He appeared in large and small saloons, the dreaded Lotus 30 and 40 sports-racing cars, even a brutish American NASCAR stocker. In some cases these were one-off outings, experiments he did not repeat, but he was intrigued by the experience.

The only road racing class he did not tackle at all seriously was long-distance sports car racing, after early forays at Le Mans and in the TT and the Nürburgring 1000 Km. Fangio drove sports cars, but seldom looked really good in them. It became a chink in his otherwise formidable armour which Jimmy perhaps shared, although in contrast his sin was one of almost complete omission. There was no doubt that Jimmy would have been as good in a soapbox as he was in a GP car, but he never proved it at sports car *Challenge Mondial* level. Like Fangio, this omission left a tiny void in his otherwise armour-plated reputation.

In 1964 he won three more GPs and two non-championship F1 events but lost a second consecutive World Championship title only by mechanical failure on the last lap of the last race, in Mexico. Yet there was no mistaking his continuing pre-eminence, as he also won a clutch of Formula 2, saloon and sports car trophies.

In 1965 he not only regained the drivers' title, but also won Indianapolis at his third attempt and, by combining domination in both road and speedway racing, perhaps became motor racing's very first truly 'World' Champion. But for that last-lap failure in Mexico the previous year this would have been his hat-trick championship season, the equivalent of Fangio in '56 – but the cookie didn't crumble for him that way.

For 1966 – first season of the new 3-litre Formula 1 – Team Lotus could only provide him with a makeshift interim car – a 2-litre Lotus-Climax – pending readiness of the definitive 3-litre BRM H16-engined Lotus 43s. All season long he battled against terrific odds, but at Watkins Glen for the money-rich United States GP his luck changed at last, and as faster runners struck trouble so he showed all his mechanical sympathy to nurse his creaking Lotus-BRM home to win.

Team had been awaiting development of the brand new Cosworth-Ford V8 engine – initially for its exclusive use – in 1967. Colin introduced it, powering the latest Lotus 49, in the Dutch GP at Zandvoort where Jimmy gave it a fairy-tale baptism to win at record speed. Ford money teamed him that year with Graham Hill, his friend and former adversary from BRM. Jim was faster, and when his car held together he won four more Grands Prix. But it did not hold together often enough to deny Denny Hulme the world title, after winning only two GPs for Repco Brabham but accumulating more points from high-scoring placings. In contrast Jimmy tended to win or bust; he won his *fifth* British GP, his fourth Dutch and his third United States and Mexican races, but it niggled him privately that someone who had won only two GPs to his four could deny him what could easily have been his fourth world title. He confided in very few, but he felt the system was somehow at fault. His well-developed sense of what was right and proper, simple sporting fairness, was mildly offended.

Right at the start of 1968 he won the South African GP to score his 25th championship-qualifying Grand Prix victory, breaking Fangio's ten-year-old career record. He followed up by completing his fifth tour of races in New Zealand and Australia to win his third Tasman Championship title and then returned expectantly to Europe via America, where a startling new four-wheel drive gas-turbine-engined Lotus was ready for what would have been his sixth Indianapolis 500.

On 7 April 1968 Jimmy was racing his uncompetitive Lotus 48 in the second round of the year's European F2 Championship, at Hockenheim in Germany. A tyre was damaged by debris on the track, it deflated at very high speed, and his car went slithering broadside into trackside trees. And he died.

Perhaps it's more significant to review the formative influences upon Jim Clark, and the personal recollections of those who worked with him, than merely to rehash the familiar story of his international career, covered so well – and so often – elsewhere.

Jim Clark was the fifth child, and only son, of a comfortably middle-class Scottish farming family, his father James, his mother Helen. He had four older sisters, Mattie, Isobel, Susan and Betty. He was born on 14 March 1936, in Kilmany, out on the east-coast Fife peninsula between the twin Firths of Forth and Tay.

When Jimmy was six, the family moved down to the village of Chirnside near Duns in Berwickshire, only a dozen miles or so from the English border. His father took over Edington Mains Farm, a sizeable spread, with 1240 useable acres plus another 200 of woodland. They raised sheep and fattened cattle, and grew whatever arable crops and vegetables might be profitable at the time. They were astute and shrewd, successful in the business of farming – sometimes to their new neighbours' envy...

Jim's father ran an Alvis Speed Twenty until wartime shortages saw it laid up and replaced by a more economical Austin 7 in which, at the age of nine, Jim had his first experience of driving. The Alvis was revived in 1946, when he was still too small to see through its windscreen and simultaneously reach the pedals. Fortunately for him, the Alvis had a hand-throttle on its steering wheel so he only needed the pedals to brake, and when necessary he would simply vanish into the basement to do so...

After three years' primary school in Chirnside, Jim attended Clifton Hall boarding prep school in Edinburgh, then entered Loretto in 1949. He proved a good sportsman, a poor student. He left at 16 to work on the family farm.

At Loretto he had already been attracted to motor racing, reading the weekly magazines and motoring books in the library. In 1948 his eldest sister Mattie had married a local farmer named Alec Calder, proud owner of a 3-litre Bentley and a Brooklands Riley. During his schooldays Jim had also been taken south to stay with relatives in Kent, and while there he saw a 500 cc motor race at nearby Brands Hatch. He was fascinated. He bought an autographed photo of Stirling Moss, but his real interest was more in the cars than the drivers.

Still an avid cricketer, he was returning one night from a match at Jedburgh when he saw the three Ecurie Ecosse C-Type Jaguars being driven in team formation out of Kelso. It was a stirring sight, a formative moment. The Winfield aerodrome circuit lay only six miles or so from Chirnside, and one day he heard that Ecosse were testing there. With two pals he cycled over to watch. The bug was nibbling into his soul. His lifelong farmer friends Billy Potts and Oswald Brewis were equally keen. When the Winfield Joint Committee lost their own aerodrome circuit they began organising races instead at another nearby airfield, Charterhall.

Following the deaths of both an uncle and grandfather within days of one another, Jim's father took on their two farms, Over Roxburgh and Kerchesters, in addition to running his own. Farming dominated family life, but Jim was already car crazy. He badly wanted a motor cycle; his parents vetoed it, but allowed him to apply for a provisional driving licence on his 17th birthday. Barely six weeks later he passed his driving test.

Father had been running a Sunbeam-Talbot 90 saloon, but now replaced it with a new Rover and handed the Sunbeam – 'BSH 510' – to his son. Young Jim quickly built a local reputation as 'a scorching driver', tearing around those wonderful, open, rolling – above all virtually *empty* – Border roads, teaching himself the finer arts...

He was keen to compete at some level, and when the local Berwick & District Motor Club ran a driving test at Winfield, it was garage owner Jock McBain who encouraged him to enter. McBain was not only the local Ford main dealer but also a prime force behind the Border Reivers racing team...

After that first driving test Jim spent the evening at Alec Calder's house, where an embarrassed telephone call from the club explained they believed he had actually won, but since he was not a member he was ineligible for an award. He reacted indignantly, and would not join the club for another year...the stubborn streak was already there.

He did occasional local rallies and driving tests, happy to be allowed to do so, confident his parents would frown on anything more serious, and dangerous. His father clearly believed this interest in motor sport was all a waste of time, and money...the Clarks were naturally careful...

Using the Sunbeam for daily transport, Jim joined the local Ednam & District Young Farmers' Club where he met Ian Scott-Watson, a budding competition driver. Jim's local reputation had preceded him. They were drawn together as kindred spirits. Jim worked on Ian's Buckler-based Bufota special, and in 1954–55 Scott-Watson rallied the first of his series of DKW *Sonderklasse* saloons, with Jim his occasional navigator.

Jim began driving too, rallying the Sunbeam. Despite his inexperience he was already faster than Scott-Watson. He autocrossed the car at Romanno Bridge, and in the early summer of 1955 competed in the major Scottish International Rally, as Billy Potts's navigator in an Austin-Healey.

A year later, in June '56, Ian Scott-Watson and Jim Clark took the former's DKW up north for an Aberdeen & District MC meeting at Crimond aerodrome. Jim was meant to be the mechanic, but as Scott-Watson recalls: 'I just took pity on him during practice and asked if he would like to have a go...his face lit up and then we went into one of these sessions where he said no, he couldn't and I said he should and he said again no, he couldn't go out on the circuit. But finally he took my crash helmet and gloves and went out for the practice session. Well, he was three seconds quicker than me on his first flying lap...I was put off racing from that moment...'

Jim was never to be noted for his decisiveness out of a car, but as the only son he never forgot his family responsibilities...Crimond was so far from Duns his parents might never hear about it. He was so excited by the prospect of racing he decided to take the chance.

'I can remember sitting in the DKW waiting for the sports car race to begin that day. I felt I was on hallowed ground because racing to me was something almost sacred that was not for me to touch. The opposition was not all that strong, but I knew I had no chance of winning and was terrified lest I made a complete fool of myself. My memories of that race are vague, but I do recall passing Peter Gordon, who was well known at that time with a highly modified Austin A90. I had heard a lot about him and here I was passing him. I only found out at the end of the race that he had broken a half-shaft, and I still finished last...'

Soon after, Scott-Watson founded the Border Motor Racing Club, with Jimmy his assistant secretary and other like-minded friends in support. They organised a high-speed trial at Beadnell, just across the border into England, the idea being to cram as many laps as possible into 30 minutes. Jimmy won classes in both his Sunbeam and Scott-Watson's DKW. He later recalled that as 'one of the best afternoon's sport I have ever had'.

Later in 1957 Scott-Watson traded in the DKW for a Porsche 1600 Super – 'UUL 442' – ex-Billy Cotton, the bandleader. Jim would recall it as being 'the car which really set me off'.

The Border MRC ran its first race meeting that September, and Jim won the BMRC Trophy handicap in Scott-Watson's Porsche.

Into 1958 he began racing seriously despite now fierce parental opposition. 'There were many rows, and events from then moved on so quickly that I was really torn apart wondering what to do...' Too many people confuse 'niceness' for 'softness'. Throughout his life, Jim Clark's sheer niceness concealed a core of steel. If he didn't want to do something, he simply would not do it, and that extended from his sporting affairs right through his personal relationships.

Jock McBain's co-operative Border Reivers team was keen to race seriously, but lacked a readily available driver. Jock's garage was only a couple of miles from

Edington Mains, and Jim spent hours there ostensibly collecting components for the
farm vehicles, while really discussing motor racing.

McBain asked Jimmy if he would drive and explained they were buying a D-Type
Jaguar – 'TKF 9' – a car prepared 'down south' by the Murkett Bros. Jim felt it would
be beyond him, a thoroughbred sports-racing car, far more powerful and faster than
anything he had yet experienced. Testing it at Charterhall 'scared me to death. It was
extremely fast…' – and irresistible.

Despite his parents' opposition, he raced the Reivers D-Type throughout 1958, with
considerable club success. Scott-Watson was now keen to go Continental, and entered
both his Porsche and the D-Type for the *GP de Spa* meeting in Belgium that May.
Shortly before making this exciting European debut, Jimmy drove the D at Charterhall, locked its brakes – terribly easy to do in a D when attempting to brake ultra-late
– and slithered off through a fence at the end of the straight…

His introduction to real Continental-style road racing at Spa then marked him for
life: 'If I had known the kind of track it was I'd never have gone. But then this was typical of Ian, without whom I'd never have tackled half the races I did, particularly in the
early days, for I had insufficient confidence in my own ability…Even then he was talking about me driving Formula 1, which to me was ridiculous at that time…'

The Reivers and Ecurie Ecosse shared the same garage at Malmedy, the larger Edinburgh team's much-modified Lister-Jaguar being driven by Masten Gregory, facing
the works Lister of the great Archie Scott-Brown. Both were heroes to young Clark,
Gregory especially, for he had recently beaten Scott-Brown with the Ecosse Lister, an
enormous feat.

Veteran driver Jack Fairman took Jimmy around the daunting *Circuit Nationale* in a
VW hire car, pointing out various features, not least the points where drivers had been
killed and injured…and there are many such points at Spa.

After practice Jimmy was left feeling very small, isolated and exposed – way out of
his depth for the big race in the D-Type. But first he drove the Porsche home to finish
fifth in the GT event.

For the big-car race, up there on the front row sat Scott-Brown, Gregory and Paul
Frère in a works Aston Martin. The start-time was 4 p.m. 'and by this time I had a
good dose of the shakes'.

From the flag, Scott-Brown and Gregory began a ferocious battle for the lead, which
ended in disaster as the works Lister crashed and burned out, Archie sustaining fatal
burns. Even without the sight of that glittering trackside fireball, Jimmy felt he was in
way over his head but later in the race he began to settle instinctively into a decent
rhythm, in tune with both car and circuit. And then Masten Gregory lapped him: 'I
was coming down to Burnenville Corner and by now I had a scrap of confidence and
felt I was really beginning to motor. The car actually felt as if it was drifting and I was
not concentrating too hard on what was coming up behind. Suddenly there was an
almighty howl of sound, a blast of wind, the whole car shook, and Masten went
steaming past like a bat out of hell. He was well in the lead with the Lister-Jaguar all
sideways, his arms crossed up and fighting the steering. I remember having this sudden

Quiet, civilised, the perfect gentleman – Clark at home in Edington Mains…picking his fingernails, of course.

twinge of shock and thinking, "To heck with this, if this is motor racing I'm going to give up now..."'

His education that day did not end there. As Frère and Bianchi stormed by and entered the Masta Straight, Jimmy snapped into their slipstreams. 'I found I was as quick as they were. Then, like an idiot, I got halfway out of the slipstream just before the kink in the middle of the straight, and the whole car was suddenly blown right across the circuit to the inside of the corner. It gave me the shock of my life, and we reckoned afterwards that I had been doing about 174 mph, which was quick considering that I had never been over 100 mph on a racing circuit until about a month before...'

Back home, Jimmy had traded in his faithful Sunbeam against a Triumph TR3 – 'RSC 190' – which he used in minor competitions. Yet another enthusiastic farming friend, Andrew Russell, acompanied him in the TR in the Border Rally, which they won, becoming a regular rally pairing.

At the final Charterhall meeting of the year, Jimmy in the Reivers' 3.4-litre D-Type on old Dunlop R3 racing tyres faced Ron Flockhart and Innes Ireland in D-Type and Tojeiro-Jaguar both entered by Ecurie Ecosse, both 3.8-litre engined and both running the latest Dunlop R5s.

It was a formative outing: 'This I think was the first time I really drove the D-Type to its limit. I had a real tussle with them that day...' He finished third behind the Ecosse pair in one event, and split them in the second.

'This gave me a great deal of confidence for I realised I could at least race with people of that stature, driving the D-Type to its limit, and still keep up...'

It's typical of this somewhat diffident, almost terminally modest character that he should recall that 'Up to then I had always had this nagging fear that I would be involved in a tight race and get so carried away with the excitement that I would drive the car too fast and go straight off the road. I was surprised, somewhat, to find that I had remained *compos mentis*, though I had been sideways a couple of times.'

Back home Mum and Dad still railed against his racing. For the first time the sport had taken him away from farming. But Jim was enjoying it hugely, and he became that year's Scottish Speed Champion.

Jock McBain was convinced of his potential, and planned to graduate into single-seater racing for 1959, buying a new Vanwall-shaped Lotus 16 for Formula 2. He arranged for Jimmy to attend a Lotus test day at Brands Hatch. The date Colin Chapman had chosen was the day after a friend of Jim's, Johnny Prentice, was to be married near London, with Jimmy his best man. It was perfect. Kismet.

None of Lotus's people appreciated that not only had Jim never driven round Brands Hatch before, he had never even sat in a single-seater racing car!

He recalled: 'It was so tight I almost made a complete nonsense of it at the very first corner. I arrived and took my foot off the accelerator and put it on what I thought was the brake and pushed. But nothing happened, for I had put my foot on the bulkhead. I stabbed about and eventually found the brake and managed to get round the corner on the grass. I remember thinking, "What would Chapman say about me if I wrote the car off on the first corner?"'

Halfway through that session, in fact, Colin had remarked to Ian Scott-Watson, 'He's not bad for a fellow who has never driven the car before,' whereupon Ian confessed what else was new to Jimmy. Colin was speechless, and more vividly impressed...

During a second session in the Type 16 Jimmy lapped very respectably in 58.9 seconds, while works driver Graham Hill clocked 56.3 for a new unofficial lap record. Immediately after Jim's final stint Graham went out again, a hub broke, the car threw a wheel, and rolled. Graham was unhurt, but Jimmy refused point-blank to have any more to do with the F2 Lotus. 'I was not going to drive anything which broke like that...'

Years later, recalling that day, Colin told me, 'The first time I ever saw Jimmy drive I was impressed – you just couldn't help it, there he was trying something completely new and going very quickly too. His times certainly made Graham's moustache bristle...'

That same day he let Jimmy try a Lotus Elite, and challenged him to a ten-lap race, himself in the Elite versus Jimmy in the Porsche with a one-lap start. Jimmy refused: 'I had the wrong tyres on and talked my way out of it...'

But he was hugely impressed with the Elite, so Ian promptly ordered one for him to race...

Within weeks, Colin was in touch to announce that the new Elite could be ready in time for Boxing Day Brands Hatch. A Christmas Eve phone call confirmed it, and late on Christmas Day the two young Scots caught the overnight sleeper from Berwick to London, collecting the car at the Green Park Hotel next morning. They arrived at Brands ready to practise, and then Jim drove a classic race against Colin's works car.

Jim recalled: 'Eventually I drew away from him a bit and I thought I was going to win, when we came up to lap a Sprite...[who] spun at Druids right in front of me, clipping the front end of my Elite...Colin nipped through and won with me second.'

McBain and the Reivers pondered plans for 1959, and chose to buy the nimble little 'flat-iron' Lister-Jaguar – 'HCH 736' – ex-Bruce Halford and Le Mans.

'The Lister taught me a great deal about racing...It was a beast of a thing...really vicious, but it was more fun than any except maybe the Aston Martins I drove later...We managed to push the driver's seat further back and my first race with the car was at Mallory Park where I had a real field day, winning three races in the Lister and one with the Elite...you could drive [the Lister] round the corners on the throttle whereas the D-Type was all stop or all go. The Lister was very much more progressive. It taught me quite a bit about brakes in that I couldn't rely on them. I had to nurse them and make them work without overheating them. The handling...was fabulous. For example at Gerards Bend at Mallory you could set the car up going into the bend hard, and get round the corner without touching the steering again. If you wanted to come out tight you just put your boot in it, the tail came round and it was a matter of driving it round on the throttle the whole way. That really taught me quite a bit about racing, particularly about controlling a car by the throttle...'

He had a very successful year, which included a quasi-works Border Reivers Elite drive at Le Mans, sharing the car with Sir John Whitmore. Colin Chapman entered it and held a driver briefing for the two young drivers the night before the race: 'This was

the first time of course I had come under the control of Colin, so to speak…his instructions were very clear and helpful…'

He found the Elite ideal for a newcomer to Le Mans – 'fast enough to be interesting but not fast enough to be all that dangerous'. It reached 142 mph down the straight, but what really staggered him was that 'the general standard of driving was not very great at all. There just aren't 120 good enough drivers to compete together at Le Mans…' Their car was dogged by starter motor trouble, lost some 2½ hours in the pits, but eventually finished tenth overall, second in class.

Scott-Watson subsequently bought the car and Jimmy raced it. He had meanwhile bought Ian's faithful 50,000-mile Porsche 1600 Super, and on occasion he sprinted it. He completed the season in the Lister and Elite, scoring his first win with the Lotus in the *Autosport* 3 Hours at Snetterton.

Hell for leather on home ground – Jimmy attacking the Scottish Bo'ness hill climb in Ian Scott-Watson's second, ex-Le Mans Lotus Elite, 1959.

The Lister was not suitable for the RAC TT at Goodwood, so in its absence David Murray of Ecurie Ecosse – the Reivers' great Scottish rivals – invited Jimmy to co-drive their latest Tojeiro-Jaguar, fresh from Le Mans, with the driver he admired so much at that time, Masten Gregory.

'Here I was in a highly competitive car with a really top-line co-driver in direct competition with the might of the Ferrari works team, the Porsche team and of course the Astons...any confidence I had was strained to the limit...'

But in practice he found two things – the car was an ill-handling dog and he was almost as quick as Masten in it. Jimmy explained: 'Every driver goes through a number of turning-points in his career...each driver builds up images within himself. Once he has cracked one image he invents another, and so progresses onwards and upwards. My particular image was Masten. During the race I found myself lapping as quick as Masten could and in this race I first realised that I might seriously compete with the idols of my schooldays...It had a profound effect on me.' He was discovering the talent within.

Their race ended when – Masten claimed – the Toj's steering failed, and the head-on impact with the bank at Woodcote Corner had a profound effect upon the car, folding it in two, and upon Masten – who was tossed clean over the bank, breaking his shoulder.

Jimmy fought a number of duels in the Elite against Graham Warner's sister car – the famous 'LOV 1'. Warner recognised the young Scot's promise and entered one of his Chequered Flag dealership team's new front-engined Gemini FJ cars for him at Boxing Day Brands Hatch. It was a dismal single-seater race debut for the future Master. After trouble in practice, a flat battery demanded a push-start and he finished well down the field. In the GT race he fought a terrific duel against 'LOV 1' until 'at Paddock Bend on the last lap, having realised I couldn't possibly overtake him, I decided to coast home. Suddenly I lost control of the Elite on the wet track, eventually hitting a bank and breaking a rear hub. This was terribly disappointing...it turned out to be my last race in one of Ian's cars. It was also my first crash...It shook my confidence for I never fully understood why I lost control...[perhaps] I had relaxed not only my speed but also my concentration...it brought home to me the necessity of concentrating from start to finish...'

Heading for trouble in 'ESH 700', Boxing Day Brands, 1959, Jimmy slides the Elite out of Bottom Bend between Graham Warner's departing 'LOV 1' and Richard Shepherd-Barron's Alfa Romeo. Last time out in a Scott-Watson car, Jimmy finally settled for second place – and promptly suffered his first racing accident...

Despite this salutary lesson, Jimmy then won his Aston Martin Formula 1 contract for 1960 – triggered through Jock McBain's long-lasting friendship with Reg Parnell, the Aston team manager. He was invited to a frosty, ice-patched Goodwood for a test day. After acclimatisation in a big 4.2-litre DBR2 sports-racer he was sent out in the DBR4/250 Formula 1 car.

'I had only once actually driven any single-seater in a race before, the Gemini FJ...the single-seater Aston was something very different. The car was big to look at, and in the cockpit I stared out on those enormous exposed wheels and tyres and thought, "This is it..."'

But the car handled little differently from old 'HCH' – the flat-iron Lister – although with its thoroughbred racing engine it felt tremendously fast, its brakes were 'fabulous and it felt a jolly good car'.

Meanwhile, Colin Chapman had floated the possibility of Jimmy driving for Team Lotus come 1960, and as the winner of the 1959 Lotuseer Trophy – for the most successful driver in his first year with a Lotus – Jim had tipped off Mike Costin, who was Lotus's engineering director, that he was testing Astons at Goodwood. So it was no coincidence that Costin arrived that day with the prototype rear-engined Lotus 18 FJ car recently debuted by Alan Stacey at Boxing Day Brands. Mike asked Reg Parnell if he minded Jim trying the new car while motor cyclist John Hartle was out in the Astons. Reg had no objection so Jimmy went out in the Lotus. He lapped in 1m 36s, some 4 seconds inside the existing FJ record. Even compared to the powerful front-engined F1 car, the new-generation rear-engined Lotus Junior 'was simply fantastic. I wouldn't have believed that any car could hold the road the way this Lotus did...The car seemed glued to the road...'

At 'Uncle Reg's' request Jimmy agreed to drive Aston Martin F1 cars when a seat should become available (in fact Maurice Trintignant and Roy Salvadori came to handle them in their sparse outings that year), but signed with Team Lotus to compete in the subsidiary classes – Formula 2 and Formula Junior. Simultaneously McBain and the Reivers had sold the Lister and replaced it with an ex-works Aston Martin DBR1/300 for major endurance events.

Now Jimmy 'had made up my mind to give racing a real try in 1960', and so he

At speed in the Reivers' elderly Aston Martin DBR1/300, Clark
acknowledges his friend Gauld...

27

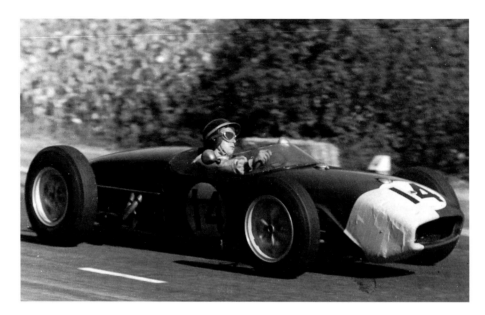

embarked upon the first of the eight seasons which fate allowed him as a full-time racing
driver. His farming responsibilities back home were assumed by his faithful steward,
Bill Campbell, and with Colin Chapman's first truly successful single-seater racing car
design – the Type 18 – Jim Clark began to carve his niche in history.

Peter Warr, later Chief Executive of Team Lotus, was at that time vigorously market-
ing the cars from the company's new factory in Delamare Road, Cheshunt,
immediately north of London. He recalls: 'I had first met Jimmy during the famous
Lotus 16 test day at the end of 1958. Jimmy amazed us all...we ran a kind of split
"works" FJ team for 1960. Jimmy's was the number one works car, prepared at the factory, while we also backed Trevor Taylor and Mike McKee – son of a famous surgeon
from Norwich – who had favoured-customer status, preparing and running their own
cars under our banner. Of course they swept everything before them, and Jimmy and
Trevor ended up sharing the British FJ Championship at the end of the year.'

In April Jim made his F2 debut in the Brussels GP only to have his engine throw a
rod after five laps. In May he shone with the Reivers' hefty Aston DBR1 in the ADAC
1000 Km sports car classic at the Nürburgring, out-sprinting Stirling Moss in the Le
Mans-type start and passing the pits second to the Maestro after a hugely impressive
first 14-mile lap. The engine finally broke its valvegear.

He tackled the *Prix Monaco Junior* in his works 18, on his first visit to the Monte Carlo
circuit, which 'suited me, being one where you have to time every corner accurately.
Half the fun I get out of racing is trying to time my cornering exactly so that I go
through smoothly with no wasted effort. Piloting the Junior was like driving in an
armchair and this just heightened the effect...' He led until a loose HT lead created a
misfire, finally finishing seventh.

Aston Martin's latest F1 cars – among the last front-engined GP 'dinosaurs' – had not been ready in time for Monaco so Jimmy had no GP debut there, but then there was talk of him running as Roy Salvadori's number two in the following Dutch GP at Zandvoort, until a quibble with the organisers over the need to qualify for start money persuaded Aston Martin to scratch their entries...

Meanwhile, Colin Chapman had entered three 2½-litre F1 Lotus 18s for that race, listing his regular number one – Innes Ireland – and Alan Stacey as team drivers, plus new boy John Surtees (just turning his attention from two wheels to four). Surtees, however, had a clashing motor cycle commitment. Aston's withdrawal left Jimmy free so Colin offered him the drive.

And so, on 6 June 1960, Jimmy made his F1 race debut in a works Lotus 18 in the Dutch GP at Zandvoort – and he was running comfortably fifth before his 18's notorious 'Lotus queerbox' transmission fell apart.

Seven days later, for the Belgian GP, Jimmy again deputised for Surtees: 'This race at Spa – like my first on that circuit – will stay with me for ever for this was one of the most tragic races in which I have competed, and if ever any one race gave me thoughts of retiring it was this one. There was a jinx on it from start to finish...'

In sister Lotus 18s both Stirling Moss and Mike Taylor crashed very badly during practice due to suspension and steering breakages. Overnight, before the race, Team's cars were checked, and both Innes' and Alan Stacey's hubs showed signs of similar failure to Moss's. New parts were fitted.

Against this background Jimmy started only his second F1 GP in a car he could not have entirely trusted on a super-fast circuit he already frankly feared. He was delayed by blocked carburettor jets, saw where Innes had spun crazily all over the road, and was perhaps feeling amused and rather more confident until 'a few laps later I was almost put off racing completely, for I was the first to arrive on the scene at Burnenville when Chris Bristow was killed in his Cooper'.

He was left with an image of a marshal dragging Bristow's body from the track, and would finish with blood on his car which 'put me off completely'.

Yet worse followed. Some laps later his team-mate Alan Stacey crashed after an apparent bird-strike in the face. His car tumbled end-over-end down into a field and burned out, the one-footed Essex driver being killed.

Jimmy finished fifth – admittedly among a depleted field – but still fifth, scoring his first two World Championship-qualifying points. It meant nothing to him, 'But I did not have much time to brood...'; the Reivers Aston was entered for Le Mans.

Again he led away from the run-and-jump start, and after a steady, intelligent race he and co-driver Roy Salvadori finished third. The shock of Spa was buried – if never to be forgotten – and Jim Clark, professional racing driver, was rapidly finding his feet.

As that season progressed he had his first F1 accident during practice for the Portuguese GP at Oporto, trying a tight line too fast on only his second lap and cannoning from a tall kerb into straw bales lining the opposite side of the road. He recalled how 'Colin was determined not to sacrifice starting money so the idea was to build a "starting money special" [for] the race.' After an all-night rebuild, Jimmy repaid the

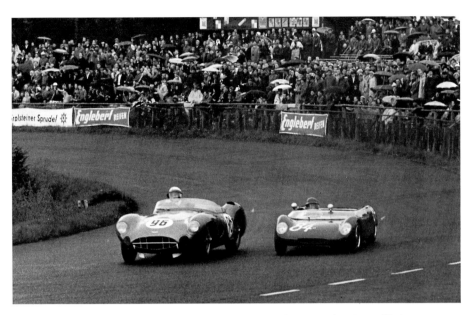

mechanics by finishing third, his best GP result of the year, despite suffering an upset tummy. Colin confirmed his place in the team for '61.

He was seeing the world. He made his American debut in the US GP at Riverside, California, and had become a graded driver, ineligible to continue in Formula Junior after just that maiden season. As Jim wrote subsequently, 'I had become accustomed to Grand Prix racing. I enjoyed it and I savoured the atmosphere which surrounded it. I was beginning to understand much more about the cars I drove, and already Colin Chapman and I were forging a bond of friendship…'

Into 1961 his newly established profession took him to New Zealand and Australia for his first Tasman series. Back in Europe he was rapidly recognised as one of the most promising of all the younger drivers, and Colin had made it clear to both his F1 pilots – Innes Ireland and Jimmy himself – that there was no No. 1 and No. 2, they were both equal within Team. But right at the end of that season – after the further trauma of the collision with von Trips at Monza – Jimmy found himself alone as Team Lotus's number one, and his old sparring partner from Formula Junior days – Trev Taylor – was number two…

Colin Chapman had abruptly – brutally – dropped Innes Ireland, only 16 days after Innes had notched Team's first-ever championship GP win at Watkins Glen. Effectively he was putting all his faith for the future in Jimmy.

Peter Warr: 'Innes had always been a rumbustious, fun-loving character, and that never sat all that comfortably with Colin. He found Jimmy far more single-minded, dedicated, and since Colin had only just given up driving himself, and had seen first-hand how Jimmy could drive, he took that gamble…and Innes was out, and Trev Taylor was in.'

In the Springbok series Jimmy won the Rand GP, Natal GP and the non-championship South African GP, while the other event – the Cape GP – fell to team-mate Trev. For Jimmy, 'I had the extra satisfaction of beating Stirling twice in two weeks on this trip, although, in fairness, my car was newer than his...'

Every great sportsman at or near his peak develops a shrewd idea of those who might threaten his position. Those with the eyes to see, whether they are man enough to acknowledge it or not, have always been able to tell early on in whose hands the future of their chosen sport might lie.

Moss was on record as having said, 'Jim Clark is the only man I fear...'

He recalls, 'I had watched Jimmy's progress with interest during the European season, as he clearly had enormous potential. He was perhaps the strongest threat to whatever position I had enjoyed since Fangio's retirement but I felt confident I could handle him, although without an equal car I might have to go some...'

In fact at Westmead in the Natal GP Stirling had to start from the back of the grid, and after pulling through to finish second behind Jimmy he wrote baldly in his diary that night: 'Couldn't make any way on him...'

Of course the real truth of motor racing is that, whatever the driver's talents, technical factors massively influence the outcome. In the case of this Moss v. Clark duel that day in Natal, the track was slippery, Moss's UDT-entered year-old car was on Dunlop D9 tyres, Clark's latest works-entered Type 21 was on D12s. While Moss's ran a 4.4:1 back axle making his engine peak at 7450 rpm down the straight, Clark's was a 4.2:1 enabling him to use seven-five...

But it was a good race and a good win for Clark and Team, a defeat for Moss, but not yet one – he knew – on even terms...

During practice for the South African GP at East London, Moss was then troubled by locking brakes because his car was fitted with small calipers which overheated and grabbed unpredictably. His team-mate Masten Gregory handed over his car with larger calipers, and Moss immediately set a quicker time.

On Christmas Eve it was water sports for the circus, Stirling teaching Jimmy to water-ski, a pastime he came to love. On Christmas night Moss was ill. Next morning out at the circuit 'I still felt lousy...my diary tells the story of the race like this: *"Had good start, Trev & Jim out-accelerated me, Jimmy spun & I had 14 sec lead. Couldn't keep him off. Too quick. My car OK but too slow...Feel lousy still..."*

'I had finished second behind Jimmy again and it was obvious to me that if I wanted to keep ahead during the coming World Championship season we would need an equal car, a Lotus 24 with a Climax V8 engine or perhaps a Ferrari V6 run for me by Rob Walker...Jimmy was that good...'

Jim Clark had indeed arrived in those two minor, now largely forgotten, South African races. His had been a meteoric rise to the top of the pack, and he would go so far in the seven years left to him that he would rewrite all of the motor racing record books.

From 1962 to his death in April 1968, Jimmy's great races are detailed so far as space allows in the captions to the accompanying photographs. But perhaps his greatest epitaph is in the deep emotion, the evident reverence, not only of his friend and mentor Colin Chapman's memory, but also of those held almost universally by all his other former colleagues...

Andrew Ferguson joined Team Lotus in 1961 after working as team manager for Cooper Cars and then for Lucky Casner's Camoradi racing team. He recalls Jimmy as not only the outstanding racing driver of his time, but also as a singularly likeable person.

'Jim Clark was a very diffident bloke, casual, just a very normal person. When he was in the works at Cheshunt he'd make a point of just poking his head into the offices to say hello to everybody. The first time I met him I'd just started there and he stuck his head round the door and said simply, "Good morning, my name's Jim Clark."

'He really was the most unassuming bloke. You never got the feeling you were in the presence of a real superstar, he was just one of the boys, one of the quieter ones, though very much one we all thought the world of. He never seemed to regard himself as anybody at all special, and that really mystified some people, especially the Americans, who like their superstars to have some air of, you know, arrogance...

'In 1965, Ford's top brass visited us at Cheshunt to discuss the new year's Indy programme. The meeting was at 10.30, say, and Jimmy burst in only about ten minutes late but terribly flustered and apologetic. We went through all the usual agenda, discussing the engine requirement and Ford's sponsorship and eventually the Ford chaps turned to Jimmy and said, "Well, all we need now is your decision; are you going to do the race for us?"

'And there was this uncomfortable silence, while Jimmy twisted in his seat and shuffled his feet and looked embarrassed which of course embarrassed us.

'And then someone asked, "What's the problem – the set-up with the engines, the money, clash of dates or what?"

'Silence.

'So we'd then recap over everything which had been discussed previously and Jimmy still sat there looking acutely embarrassed, until he just quietly said, "Ahem – well, to be perfectly honest, it's my mother..."

'"Your *mother?*" the Ford guys gasped.

'"Yeah – she always worries about me when I do Indy because she's heard so many terrible stories about the place..."

'Remember, this was the man who would win the race that year, but he just subordinated his own interests to what he thought might be the right thing to do...How his mum felt when he was driving at Indy really mattered to him...

'For many years it simply didn't strike me just how great Jim was. He *never* behaved like the great superstar he became.

'He was always chewing his fingernails. Sitting thinking, with his fingertips always up to his mouth, was Jimmy's typical pose.

'He was completely mesmerised by Colin. The Old Man had this incredible gift of making naturally diffident, perhaps slightly withdrawn people come into their own.

He had this awesome "you can do it" approach. He'd just tell people who perhaps were not very experienced or self-confident to go off and do something extraordinary. He would place enormous responsibility on their shoulders and somehow they'd rise to the occasion and just do it. I think that from the beginning a lot of this rubbed off on Jimmy too. The confidence which Colin placed in him actually made Jimmy rise to match it. I think it made him realise he really was as good as Colin thought he was...

'And they really were great mates. For years Colin and Jimmy would always share a twin-bedded room at races. Just think of that – the team chief sharing the same room with his number one driver! Colin could have the benefit of a 24-hour debrief if he wanted it. He always used to take great interest in his drivers. He'd always rush about and make sure they were all in bed and fed and comfy.

'Jimmy just accepted all that until well towards the end. Even then he'd always make sure he stayed at the same hotel if not actually in the same room, so as not to upset Colin.

'It's amazing, isn't it? You can't imagine that happening these days. For years through the Sixties we might report to Colin's room for an early-morning meeting and there'd be Jimmy in the bathroom shaving and Colin sitting on the bed talking job-sheets or something and they'd be bawling instructions at each other...

'Jimmy was always very conscious of doing the right thing by Colin. One year we were flying back from qualifying at Indy, straight after Jimmy had won the Belgian GP at Spa in torrential rain. He and I were sitting together, with Colin in the row behind. It was the first chance I'd had to talk to him about his drive at Spa, which was a circuit we all knew he didn't like. I said to him, "That was great, wasn't it?" and as usual he was nibbling his fingernails – waiting for the grub, I suppose – and he said, "Yeah, great, but it was a bit tricky, I was quite lucky really..." and then he went quiet.

'I realised he was trying to tell me something, so I asked, "How d'you mean?" and he explained, "For three-quarters of the way the gear lever kept popping out, and I was having to drive the thing one-handed. It was very tiring, a bit bloody dangerous too..."

'So I said, "That's the trouble with you. No one will ever get to hear about that. Fangio used to have a problem like that and he'd talk about it and the press would make a big thing of it and we'd all fall over and say, 'Cor, Fangio, what a man,' but you just keep it all to yourself. If we could put out a press release telling the true story about problems like that it would do wonders for your image."

'And he just looked alarmed and said, "Oh no, we could never do that. We don't want to upset Colin!"

'That was typical Jimmy.'

Peter Warr recalls how 'The extraordinary thing about Jimmy was how such a brilliant racing driver could be so indecisive out of a racing car. He was a sensationally quick driver on the public road. He just loved driving cars. But he could get himself befuddled through this extraordinary indecisiveness. His record for the drive between his farm at Duns and our factory at Cheshunt was only about four hours – which was just incredible – but apparently there was some kind of fork not far from home where he could never quite decide whether it was quicker to take the route to the left or the

one to the right, and two or three times while he was sitting there unable to make up his mind he went straight off onto the vee and crashed instead! Of course you've got to set this against the fact that he was probably doing some enormous speed at the time, but generally he was an absolute driving natural.'

Another time Andrew recalls: 'I used to handle Jimmy's accident claims, and he kept me busy. One time Jimmy was going off, I think to London airport, in the Ford Galaxie with Trevor Taylor. I had been leaning out of my office window talking to them as they got into the car at the front of the works and then I was just idly watching Jimmy nose it out of the entrance through the row of parked cars at the roadside when I spotted this chap coming along on what turned out to be a 1928 Royal Enfield. He was wearing a Land Army girl's greatcoat and a leather flying helmet, and just as he reached where Jimmy was about to pull out in the Galaxie Jimmy finally made up his mind and *went*, and *bang* this poor chap hit him...

'I thought, "Oh no, more paperwork," but Jimmy made sure the motor cyclist was all right and then I think said to Trev Taylor, "You drive, I keep having accidents..."

'The funny thing was – I think it was that same trip – the Galaxie was an automatic and they then got themselves stuck in a traffic jam on the Great North Road. Trev was sitting there chatting to Jimmy, getting thoroughly bored with the whole thing, when he absent-mindedly gave the throttle a big blip.

'And of course the auto took up and the Galaxie slammed straight forward into the chap in front, and Jimmy creased up laughing and that meant even more paperwork for me...

'Sometimes when they were in separate cars, dicing against one another on the open road, Jimmy would get very upset indeed with Colin. The classic occasions were when they were driving from Indy out to Weir Cooke airport, with Colin really taking chances and carving up Jimmy in their big Ford sedans. When we got to the airport Jimmy rushed across to Colin and bawled at him, "You bloody dangerous fool!" He meant it, too, but it would soon dissipate and they always remained the best of friends...'

Trevor Taylor, Jimmy's team-mate in Junior and Formula 1 in 1960–63, told me long ago that 'I have never forgotten Jimmy – you couldn't – I've always used my image of him as my measure of a man. He was a great person – in all kinds of ways...

'Really his class was obvious even when we were in Formula Junior together with the 18s. I always got the impression that he was never really trying hard to set his times. He was never in trouble, he was always in control. I always had to work harder to go as fast.'

When they were teamed together, and Trev endured some difficult days and escaped unscathed from a sequence of shattering accidents, Jimmy was always concerned for him. 'He was always asking if there was anything he could do to help, generally asking how you were doing. He never held back any information as far as I can recall. And I don't think he ever had a bad word for anyone. He was the most even-tempered bloke you could hope to meet...'

Lotuses were regarded as frail, frangible cars during that period but Trevor says: 'I

27 April 1963 – Aintree 200. Although Team Lotus number two drivers were often reckoned to receive a raw deal, Team was a happy place through much of the Jim Clark period. He and his old FJ sparring partner Trev Taylor got on particularly well, perhaps despite times like this when Jim's 25 with experimental fuel injection faltered, and Trevor was brought in to swap cars. Even before mechanic Ted Woodley has stepped clear, the genuine Tiger in Clark's make-up has the clutch home and rear wheels spinning! Car '4' finished third – Trevor in '3' was seventh – and Jim left the lap record 0.6s inside his pole position time, at over 96 mph. They had swapped like this before, to win the non-championship Mexican GP the previous November.

think there was only one time at Oulton Park in 1960 that he ever mentioned any worries about the cars to me, and that was after I'd had a shunt when something broke. He
never really worried at all – he had enormous faith in Colin…and when I followed him
on a circuit he often did things with the cars which just took your breath away – not
at all because they were spectacular or hairy, but just because they were so smooth, so
relaxed and so *fast*…He never looked as if he *had* to hurry…'

You could see that from the trackside. Finesse is the word, you sensed rather than
could see the fine, instantaneous rhythm of corrections and inputs he was applying.
The apple-green Lotus, patched or striped in white and yellow with its calm, relaxed
driver, reclining there in Chapman's favoured hammock seat, barely visible beneath
his Scots-blue helmet (often Leston peakless in early days, later normally white-
peaked, or very rarely blue-peaked). Early on, he customarily wore pale-blue Dunlop
overalls; later as Team adopted Firestone tyres the first fireproof Nomex type, cream
with red piping and his name woven in script over the breast pocket. Through his
champion years he favoured Bell helmets, later – from the start of 1967 – changing to
Buco. His early peakless crash-hat caused some hilarity around '62–63 when the first space
flights were hot news.

Andrew Ferguson: 'The only time I recall Jimmy having a serious sense of humour
failure was over a photograph pinned behind the door of my tiny office at Cheshunt.
Just the way the photographer had caught him made him look facially rather like a
monkey and, with his peakless helmet and the interest of the time in pioneering space
flight, some wag had written under it something like "Next time you go into orbit,
we'll hold your banana."

'Jimmy was in my office one day and happened to notice this and he really didn't
think it was funny at all. He was always – well, particularly in the early years – pretty
strait-laced and proper, though he never pushed it, but in fact when he saw this picture
and its caption he took *great* offence – just caught him on an off-day, I suppose – and
it was then that he said, "The trouble with you people is that you just take me for
granted. I'm such a treasure, you'll miss me when I'm gone…"

'And you know, when I think about that now, he was absolutely right…

'He was so much part of us, part of Team, that we really did just assume he'd *always*
be around. And then one day he wasn't around any more, and we really did appreciate
what a treasure he had been, and what we had all lost…

'One time there was this extraordinary thing going on with some conman posing as
Jim Clark, charging up hotel rooms for himself and his girlfriends and then leaving the
bills unpaid. They were then sent through to me at Lotus. I asked Jim about it and he
swore blind he'd never been there. But it happened again, and again, and finally we called in the police and it was all getting quite serious…The police investigated and eventually told us they were looking for someone with curly ginger hair.

'We told Jimmy this and he paused, and stared at me' – at Andrew's curly ginger hair
– 'and I suddenly realised he wasn't joking when he said slowly, "That sounds just like
you!"'

It was not, of course, but for at least one moment the cautious, earnest Scot in Jimmy
really thought it could have been…

Two great drives. Above: *5 August 1962 – German Grand Prix, Nürburgring. Clark hurled his Lotus 25 around the Nordschleife like never before after muffing the start. Waiting on the grid in heavy rain he had been holding his goggles away from his face to prevent them misting up and forgot to switch on his fuel pumps after starting the engine. As the flag fell his Climax engine's carburettors ran dry and his engine stopped. He drove like fury to catch the leaders, eventually settling for fourth place. In retrospect that error cost him the world title.*

Team's chief mechanic throughout most of Clark's eight seasons was quiet, capable Jim Endruweit: 'Jim Clark was not a funny man, he wasn't the kind of chap you remember as being a great fun-loving practical joker, not like Graham Hill, for instance. No – Jimmy was very polite, very friendly, but very quiet…a civilised man, a gentleman. There was no show. He was almost unnoticeable, and very pleasant with it. The world was divided naturally into gentlemen and others and you always felt that Jimmy could be relied upon utterly; he was naturally one of nature's gentlemen, always pleasant, always polite, all the proper civilised things. He had very obviously been very well brought up.

'He very rarely threw a tantrum. He and Graham Hill, for instance, were really opposite ends of the spectrum; Graham would be effing and blinding, one of the lads, giving us fearful rollickings if things went wrong, do this, do that…Then Jimmy – nibbling his fingernails – would quietly ask, "Would you mind doing this?" or "If it's not too much trouble, could you possibly do that?"

'One time, at Rouen or Pau perhaps, we had new centre-lock wheels and for some reason in practice the wheels kept working loose, which isn't a nice thing to happen. He came in and we snugged them up but it happened again. And the second time he came in, he wasn't at all happy and he said, "What are you doing? Are you trying to kill me?" and he meant it, real venom, and because that was so unusual we really took it to heart. That was one of the *very* few times he was anything but perfectly pleasant. And he never apportioned blame if something went wrong…

'Graham would just explode, he'd shout and yell and want somebody's guts for garters. You had to be a chameleon to cope with the two of them…

'But what a driver!

'At the Ring when he stalled on the grid and went off late in appalling weather' – 1962 German GP – 'he began pulling back great chunks of time lap after lap against Graham Hill, Dan Gurney and John Surtees, all going like the clappers for the lead. Jimmy was gaining minutes a lap on them. It was incredibly exciting to watch, just fantastic, and then suddenly the gap was a little bit longer and then we realised he'd backed off and the excitement was over.

'After he finished and came in and got out of the car, we asked him, "Why did you back off like that?" and I remember he just said, "Nothing wrong with the car. I just frightened myself fartless and settled for fourth…"

'It was most unlike Jimmy to say anything at all vulgar – apart from the occasional "bloody" – so that was a measure of the fright he'd given himself…He was a wonder.

'I always think his most brilliant drive was at Silverstone in the '65 British Grand Prix when we fitted the new flat-plane crank Climax engine for the race, taking a calculated gamble on its greater oil consumption. Towards the end he was way in the lead when he suddenly came swishing out of Woodcote Corner past the pits with his engine dead and we thought, "Oh no – we've lost it," and then suddenly the engine burst into life and he rushed by sounding all right. He did it again on the next lap, and the next, and coming past us he was right down in the cockpit and just a little thumb came up to show he believed he had everything under control. He did that for five laps, and then the last time he came round Woodcote everything was running on full song and he won by a very small margin.

'Afterwards we told him we'd seen his thumbs-up and he said, "Yeah, I knew what I was doing. I noticed the oil pressure dropping through the long right-hander so I thought it'll be OK if I switch off the engine and coast until the car's running straight again" – to wash remaining oil back towards the pressure pump intake – "and then I'll switch on again..."

'He was no mechanic by any stretch of the imagination but he had this *tremendous* feel for his machinery.

'At Rouen there was an historic car race; he was lent an ERA during practice and he went off in it at a rare old pace and the owner was looking worried, but when Jimmy brought it back it wasn't even sweating – it was as if it had just been given a gentle warm-up...That was his touch.

'One time testing the dreaded Lotus 30 at Snetterton the place suddenly went all silent and we went rushing off to find him parked on the exit to the hairpin. He said, "I think there's something loose at the back, so I stopped." We looked around it, and found one of the driveshafts was about to fail. It hadn't yet failed, but it was about to...We looked at each other and thought, "Cor – how did he pick that?"'

Another time at Snetterton, testing an Indy Lotus 38 – fitted for road-circuit use with a Lotus 30-style ZF transaxle instead of the normal Indy Hewland – the late Lotus designer Maurice Phillippe recalled: 'In Cheshunt days it was normal for Colin and Jim to fly to test sessions from the grass airfield at Panshanger, and I usually went along as a passenger with Colin in his Twin Comanche, Jimmy travelling in his own single-engined version...at Snetterton after a few laps Colin suggested we view Jim's progress from the bridge at the esses...Approaching the esses Jim hit full revs in fourth and then notched into fifth. At the critical turn-in point the tyres protested and the car went into a lurid spin and disappeared under the bridge...Colin yelled at me, "This is going to be a big one!" as we ran down the bridge ramp...

'We could see no sign of driver or car. Following the black tyre marks we realised they changed to grey at one point during the spin, and then the car had changed direction to pass through a gap in the earth bank, only some twenty feet wide. On the other side, on the tarmac, was the completely undamaged car. Jimmy was out of the cockpit, looking sheepish and embarrassed. He admitted he'd made a mistake...we suspected he'd seen us and was going to give us a masterly display but the Firestone Indy tyres hadn't done enough laps to give sufficient grip.

'I was intrigued how Jim had managed to get off the brakes at the crucial moment in the spin so the car changed direction and went neatly through the gap in the bank. Jimmy agreed this was what he'd done to save the car and himself. I felt a little sceptical, but there was the evidence, on the road surface.

'Then, later in the day, he was out again and it all went quiet. We raced over to the esses and again there was Jim with the same embarrassed expression, and the car parked in an almost identical position – same tyre marks, same change of direction, and the car safely parked in the gap in the bank!'

You see, he had magical skill; truly magical.

Mechanical sympathy was a major factor in the instinctive Clark 'game plan'. He habitually wore his tyres, his brakes, his gearbox, his engine less than other, slower, lesser men and even in the underpowered 1½-litre formula could be spectacular – as here – although his cars' transition in cornering-stance through a curve was always notably, incredibly smooth, flowing – a dynamic art at the highest level.

Lotus ran Dunlop tyres during most of the Clark period and their tyre technicians certainly thought so, they had the wear-rate figures to prove it. Alec Meskell – heading Dunlop's comps department today – was a tyre engineer who worked closely with Team and Jimmy. He appreciated how Jack Brabham's habitual tail-out driving style wore his rear Dunlops quicker than his fronts, while John Surtees and Dan Gurney both wore fronts faster than rears. Jimmy was different, Jimmy was unique – he wore all his tyres evenly, while using less rubber than any competitive contemporary.

Alec Meskell: 'Jim Clark had this startling ability to lap quicker whenever he wanted. We could spend a day tyre testing, select what he felt were the best tyres, and then he'd go out again on the basic control set and lap quicker still! Technically, that was pretty exasperating, but he'd just shrug and smile that embarrassed smile and look as if he couldn't help it – he didn't know how or why he'd lapped quicker on what should have been a slower set of tyres. He never looked as if he was trying, that was the other thing – he never looked untidy and his tyre wear and temperatures were always lower than Graham's, for instance. He always seemed to adjust his driving to whatever the car or the tyres demanded – he was just naturally, apparently effortlessly, quick.'

In the excellent autobiography which Jimmy penned with his journalist friend Graham Gauld, he gave a little insight into his driving: 'most people run deep into a corner before turning the wheels to go round. In this way you can complete all your braking in a straight line, as everyone recommends you do, before setting the car up for the corner; but I prefer to cut into the corner early and even with my brakes on to set up the car earlier. In this way, I almost make a false apex because I get the power on early and try to drift the car through the true apex and continue with this sliding until I am set up for the next bit of straight...'

This is almost word for word the old Moss method which set the pinnacle standard BC – 'Before Clark'. Stirling appreciated that braking in a straight line and then locking into the corner was substituting one tyre loading – braking – for another – cornering. As he had honed his technique through the later 1950s he perfected the art of balancing both loads simultaneously, braking later and maintaining it right to the apex, where he had the sensitivity almost instantaneously to replace the combined loads of braking and cornering with those of acceleration and cornering. Jim Clark could do the same.

Because of the change of Grand Prix formula it could be argued that he perfected his art in the underpowered machinery of 1½-litre racing. But consider his showing in the 4.7-litre and 5.3-litre Ford V8-powered Lotus 30 and 40 sports cars and the 7-litre Galaxie saloon and then the 4.2-litre Indianapolis Lotus-Fords, and that potential stricture collapses.

In terms of sheer driving talent, skill and technique the natural regal progression really does stand up – Fangio to Moss to Clark, each the emperor within his era.

New Zealand mechanic Leo Wybrott – today McLaren International's works manager – joined Team in 1964 and perhaps most vividly recalls Jimmy's braking judgement, as exemplified in the '66 Dutch GP at Zandvoort: 'That was the first season of the new 3-litre formula. Our latest BRM H16-engined thing wasn't ready so Jimmy

was driving instead his 33 with the 2-litre Climax V8. He was in a terrific battle with the 3-litre Repco Brabhams when he suddenly peeled off the main straight and hurtled into the pit. From absolutely flat-strap on the straight he stopped *bang* in front of us, dead centre, perfect.

'It was stunning, but we had no time to admire it at that moment. The engine's vibration damper was coming apart, it had rubbed a hole in the water pump casing and let the water out. We topped it up and off he went, like a rocket. It was his fantastic accuracy which really stuck in my mind – specially considering the way drivers overshoot their marks on even scheduled tyre stops today...'

In the Tasman Championship one year, Alan McCall recalls how as Team mechanic he sat spellbound in a bar at Longford listening to Jimmy and Jackie Stewart on what makes a racing driver tick: 'Both agreed fear is vital. They needed to feel fear in a racing car to heighten their perceptions, so that everything seemed to them to be happening slower, which in relative terms made their reflexes faster. That's where their amazing car control came from. Jimmy said the only times he'd got into real trouble in a racing car were when he had relaxed. He'd certainly get really tight before a race, you know...really tense and screwed up.'

Alan was also witness to an extraordinary scene at Indy when nothing had gone right for the team until final qualifying was upon them. 'We'd been doing terrible things to the cars, Dave Lazenby was cutting-and-shutting rocker arms to change the suspension geometry – welding them back together behind closed doors. It was all highly illegal, and still the cars were no good. And eventually Colin called us all together and delivered a brilliant, step-by-step analysis of everything we'd done and tried during practice and testing. He made a point of crediting each of us with some contribution to progress made, but as he went on it slowly dawned on us that he was making no mention at all of Jimmy. And then you realised he was saying in effect that 'We've done all we can and the car still isn't quick, so clearly the problem is the guy in the cockpit...' And we really started to glance at each other, and at Jimmy, and were shifting around in embarrassment. Colin was going on and on, saying nothing directly, but Jimmy was there getting redder and redder in the face, not taking his eyes off Colin. It was awful to watch.

'But it worked. He went out, put his neck on the line and qualified faster than the car was able…It had been Colin's way of winding him up; astonishingly brutal – I'm sure it was undeserved – and they must have had words about it afterwards in private, but we were so far gone that only Jimmy at his best could save us, and Colin had really pumped him up…'

Moss and later Jackie Stewart spun money from their reigns. Jimmy was different, he simply was not adjusted that way. He never seemed particularly interested in his market value, he drove for the love of it, and although he was obviously a high earner he never came close to cashing in fully on his status, although as a good Scot he was certainly never careless with his cash.

Andrew: 'We regularly used a Chinese restaurant in Waltham Cross, and over one two-week period Jimmy was living in his flat in London and coming into the factory every day, so I took him to the restaurant for lunch, paid the bill, and claimed it back on my expenses. Then Colin demanded to know how it was that I was charging up my lunches every day, what the hell was going on?

'Lunch there cost six shillings each, and I always used to leave a sixpenny tip, so paying for Jimmy's as well meant 13 shillings, including a shilling tip. When I told Colin I was paying for Jimmy he told me, "He can pay for his own bloody lunch, we're not made of money!"

'Next time we went out I told Jimmy I'd got into trouble and couldn't pay for his lunch today. So I put down my six shillings and he put down his and then I added sixpence as my half of the tip. And Jimmy said, "What's that for?" and I told him, and he changed the subject! He kept his sixpence…That was typical…

'He did a series of articles in the *Daily Express* and at one point the prize money he'd won at Indy was mentioned but he added, "Of course it's not all clear money because I have many expenses to cover, including the motel laundry bill…"

'We had a great laugh about that because here we were with about a quarter of a million pounds – an enormous sum for those days – devoted to the Indy programme for him, and he was earnestly bleating about how hard it was to be faced with a three-dollar laundry bill!'

If one asked Colin or Andrew or most of Team Lotus's hierarchy if the relationship between Team and Jimmy had ever changed, this recollection seems to speak for them all: 'Yes, the relationship did change from 1960 to 1968. It got better and better, it was a constant improving curve.'

Andrew: 'It got even better in '67 when Graham Hill joined. We used to pay Jimmy on a three months in advance basis, and we'd add an allowance for his probable winnings and bonuses – we had that much confidence in him – then settle up properly at the end of the period. When Jimmy got his first payment of '67 after Graham had joined he called me up and said, "Bloody hell, Andrew! Colin's going to get a Christmas card from me this year, he's raised my pay!"

'He was as excited as a kid at Christmas, but he never haggled with us over his retainer, though early on he and I would giggle over late payment of cheques: "typical bloody Lotus", he'd say. Later he had financial advisers who chased us, but he never really seemed to appreciate what could have been his market value – he was never money-driven, not in what you might call the Jackie Stewart sense.'

Peter Warr: 'Jimmy was an absolute driving natural, but he was a natural person, no pretence at all…he was a thoroughly nice guy and he hardly changed, although he was incredibly shy at first, and when he really began to shine it was as if he couldn't grasp it. He never made much of it, and he couldn't believe the adulation.

'He found financial matters distasteful – he and Colin would talk it over and he'd always say OK – but in '67 when he was advised to become a tax exile he had to get involved and commercialism really rubbed him up the wrong way. He never really adjusted to it. He didn't chase the money…'

Andrew: 'All that had happened when Jimmy's pay was raised for '67 was that Graham had done a pretty good deal with Ford to drive for us, and as equal number one of course Jimmy got the same – and for him it was a massive increase.

'But when Graham joined us I told him, "Now you're with Team Lotus you've got to fly economy just like the rest of us," and he didn't like that at all. It was standard practice for us, we never paid first class *anywhere*. And when somebody like Ford bought the tickets and sent Colin or Jimmy first class, the first thing they would both do was to rush round to the airline office, swap the first class tickets for economy and pocket the cash…

'One time between races in the States, Graham and Jimmy stayed together in Las Vegas, and Graham of course took Jimmy to the Casino. Jimmy phoned me about something afterwards and I asked how it was going – and all he could talk about was "That bloody Graham! He's nuts, you know. We went to the Casino the other night and he took a *thousand* dollars with him to play the tables!" I asked him how much he'd taken and he said, "Oh, I thought ten dollars would be enough, then I couldn't get into trouble." And I asked what had happened to his ten dollars and he told me triumphantly, "I've still got it!"'

By January 1967 Jimmy's earnings were already high enough for his financial advisers to suggest he become a tax exile, and nominally at least he became based in Bermuda while using a Continental base in a Paris flat belonging to his friend Jabby Crombac, founder of *Sport Auto* magazine and a long-time faithful Lotuseer.

Jabby recalls how meticulously Jimmy read the motoring press – seizing on even the mildest error. He insisted upon perfect detail. When David Benson ghosted his columns for the *Daily Express* Jimmy had total control of drafting. 'If he said he was doing 149 mph and I wrote 150 mph he would strike it out and insist it was only 149…Near enough simply wasn't good enough.'

Jabby recalled: 'He was beginning to become very cosmopolitan. Obviously he had travelled worldwide, and he reacted well to living in Paris. He liked French food. He was very fond of French oysters, and we usually ended up at a seafood restaurant…'

Jimmy would drop in to *Sport Auto* editorial and commandeer a tiny office, spending

all day there catching up on reading the motoring magazines, intent upon accuracy and the errors he inevitably found.

By that time he was coming to terms with his new status and learning progressively how to enjoy it. With Jabby he became more relaxed, more cosmopolitan. He was obviously an attractive man and he had several girlfriends, but Sally Stokes was tops and they were together for quite a time. But he made it clear that marriage was incompatible with a continuing racing career. Racing won the day, and the lovely Sally eventually married Dutch racing driver and businessman Ed Swart. Jimmy was always ferociously – but quietly – independent and he could never accept any need to answer to anybody for his actions.

When he won the non-championship Madrid GP at Jarama in '67 with Graham second in the sister Lotus 49, they had a terrific party in a local club, Graham dancing the Flamenco and Jimmy with another girl in tow. Next morning Andrew and Jimmy flew to Paris on a Boeing 707 and 'we were invited up onto the flight deck and the crew said we'd obviously had a good party the night before. We were puzzled how they knew and they showed us the local Spanish newspaper which had a big splash on it with photos of Jimmy and his bird. When we arrived in Paris the first thing he did was to buy ten or twelve Paris postcards and write greetings on them all, sign them, and then post them off to various girlfriends worldwide...

'He really was coming out of his shell...'

During this period Jim began buying clothes which were tailor-made instead of off-the-peg, something he would never have done before. He let his hair grow rather longer, over his collar, and one colleague recalls how in a Parisian restaurant 'he actually seemed to enjoy being recognised, he'd greet people and engage in comfortable conversation with anyone…that was new, he would never have been so open in earlier years.'

Typical of this period was Leo Wybrott's experience with Jimmy in the final three of his five Tasman series, 1966–7–8: 'Initially Jimmy was very relaxed on the Tasman tours – you've heard all the stuff about him liking New Zealand because of the outdoor life and the way much of it is very like Scotland; we certainly enjoyed the "*après*-race", if you like, and the atmosphere was a kind of glorified club racing – there were usually just us two mechanics, Jimmy and the car representing Team. But it was noticeable that as he became more famous so the demands upon his time increased, and eventually, in '68, he was operating more or less in a team management role as well as driver and he had a lot to do with fighting the new Gold Leaf Team Lotus advertising through the Australian racing authorities, who really took a dim view of it, and he was less relaxed all round than the old Jim we knew.

'My first Tasman was in 1966 with the 4-cylinder Lotus 39. It was just Jimmy, Ray Parsons and me, and Ray as the senior mechanic acted more or less as the boss and Jimmy was "only" the driver. It was kind of "all boys together" and we shared rooms, birds and beer. Jimmy loved water-skiing and we did a lot of it. Back there again in '67 with the 2-litre V8, Alan McCall and I looked after the car and Jimmy did a little more on the managerial side until finally in '68 we had the 49s and Graham came down to Australia and we ended up with myself, Dale and Roger Porteus and then Bob Sparshott to run the two cars. In successive Tasmans Jimmy progressively had less free time; he was in great demand for various functions, he had more responsibility on his shoulders and it was hardly surprising he seemed a little less approachable, a bit more tetchy. One time we were late and missed the start of practice and he was super-cheesed-off with that – it was the first time I had ever seen him really annoyed.

'In one quiet moment we were talking about the future. He knew I was coming back to England to get married and I told him I didn't think I could keep going to the races, and he made noises about starting up something of his own to do with racing, and there could be a job there for me – a managerial type of thing which wouldn't entail attending all the events. It wasn't very clear – I can't clearly recall the details – but I'm pretty sure he was planning for the future; perhaps something was going to change? He was certainly changing, or being made to change by the circumstances surrounding him…but he certainly seemed more pressured by commercialisation…'

Privately, his family would admit they could no longer seriously picture Jimmy simply retiring from racing and returning to run the farm. He had become a citizen of the world. He was learning to enjoy his celebrity. Andrew: 'He'd have been something to do with racing had he lived, but it's almost as if racing was so much his life he would have been unequipped to do anything else…'

Back in Europe after the '68 Tasman races he drove the Formula 2 Lotus 48 at

Barcelona, being rammed from behind by Ickx's Ferrari on only the second lap. Ford were keen for him to drive Alan Mann's new P68 prototype coupé in the BOAC 500 at Brands Hatch on 7 April, but the offer was rather vaguely handled and offended Jimmy's somewhat Presbyterian sense of proper dealing. Andrew Ferguson: 'Early in '68, after the Tasman, he tested the new turbine car at Indy and got very excited about it; he said he was really looking forward to racing it. I was on my way home and Jimmy tracked me down on the phone to my hotel room in New York, and called about the clash of dates between the F2 race at Hockenheim and the BOAC sports car race at Brands Hatch.

'He said he definitely wanted to go to Hockenheim in preference to the Mann ride at Brands because he'd had the F2 commitment on his programme for a long time, and he said he wasn't very interested in going to Brands because Mann's organisation didn't seem very bright: "They said they would send me details and confirmation but nothing's appeared at all."

'And so he made his choice...'

Ask Jim Endruweit about the '68 F2 team and he will think back, and hesitantly explain: 'The 48s were not good cars.' Ask him why and the answer is flat, and simple.

'They were not good cars because Jim could not win in them.

'And if he could not win, there was something wrong with the car. He was always quite philosophical about racing them. He'd do the best he could, then away to the next meeting...

'At Hockenheim the cars were not good. He was reasonably cheerful, it was just another weekend's racing, and a rather unimportant one at that...

'Then early in the heat he failed to come round, which in itself was unusual. There were a couple of young girls in the pits acting as interpreters, and they went away and asked race control what had happened and then came back to tell us there'd been a shunt and Jimmy had been taken away in an ambulance. I was taken to a hospital miles away. We had been told he was alive but fairly seriously injured. We sat waiting in the hospital. The Germans were very kind and brought us lots of coffee, but then someone asked if I'd like a brandy and I went queasy, you know, and thought, "Oh Christ, no" – and then they told me...

'They asked if I would go and formally identify him. And I did that. He wasn't all messed up or anything. There wasn't really a mark on him, but he had a fracture of the lower left skull...and then I made the phone calls...I called the Old Man, who'd taken a rare weekend off in Switzerland – and I called Jimmy's father...

'Jim was one of a kind in every way...he really was a pretty special person. Most of the lads would have done anything for him, and he would repay you by winning in the car you built for him. If he couldn't win with it, then there was usually something else at fault. There was never any question about his skill, or his commitment. He always made the best possible use of what you provided for him. He never had an off-day, he never seemed uninterested. He was the best driver, and the best person, I've ever known...'

JIM CLARK OBE
1936 – 1968

A Portfolio

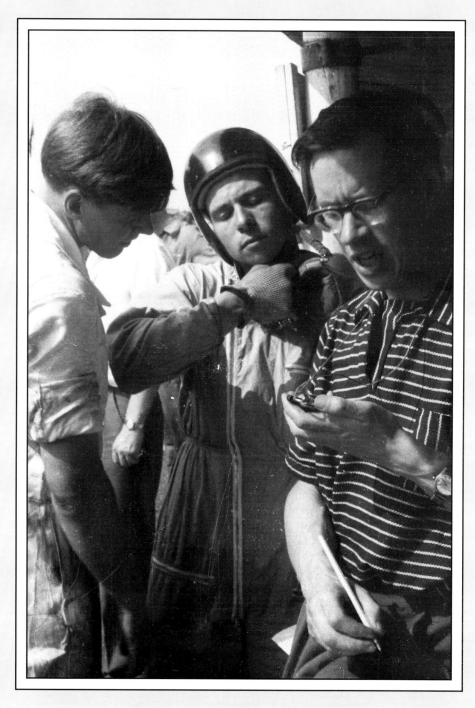

*Novice – Ian Scott-Watson announces the latest lap time, young Jim
fresh from the car removes his helmet and Team Lotus mechanic – later
Lotus Racing Manager, and much later Cosworth Engineering's field
manager – Dick Scammell checks the list; Dutch GP, Zandvoort, 1960.*

19 June 1960 – Belgian Grand Prix, Spa-Francorchamps. Jim locks the 2½-litre Lotus 18 into La Source hairpin above the pits during his overshadowed drive into fifth place and his first two World Championship points.

16 July 1960 – British Grand Prix, Silverstone. It wasn't all roses; fast-circuit nose on his works Lotus 18, Jimmy combats understeer while running as high as third before the left-front suspension collapsed and he lost seven laps having it rebuilt. He finally finished 17th – and last – in his first home Grand Prix, an event he would ultimately win five times.

3 April 1961 – Pau Grand Prix. Jim Clark's maiden Formula 1 race win, in the traditional Easter Monday round-the-town event, saw him lead from start to finish, holding off World Champion Jack Brabham in the opening stages until the Australian struck trouble, and finally beating that other established star Jo Bonnier's private Scuderia Colonia Lotus 18.

6 August 1961 – German Grand Prix, Nürburgring. The great race in which Moss's obsolescent Walker team Lotus 18/21 held off the more powerful works 'Sharknose' Ferraris of Phil Hill and 'Taffy' von Trips to score Stirling's 14th and final Grande Épreuve victory. Best of the rest that day was young Clark, here in his fourth-placed works Lotus 21.

Clark's first World Championship-qualifying Grand Prix victory came on 17 June 1962, in the Belgian event, where else but at Spa. Here he is, rifling his Lotus 25 through Les Combes corner high on the top of the ridge after Eau Rouge. His engine had failed in practice, he started from row five of the grid and led from lap nine to the finish, setting a new 1½-litre lap record en route to win from the Hills, Graham in the BRM, Phil in the Ferrari. On the control tower balcony after the race, Jim was self-effacing in triumph, Colin Chapman happy, almost admiring…

6 June 1963 – Belgian Grand Prix, Spa-Francorchamps. Leading from start to finish Jim won the Ardennes race for the second consecutive time, despite the last seven laps being run in this torrential downpour. Jimmy's fastest lap averaged 132.47 mph!

23 June 1963 – Dutch Grand Prix, Zandvoort. Invincibility – Clark and the Lotus 25 started from pole position, led throughout, set fastest lap – raising the seaside circuit's lap record to over 100 mph for the first time – and won after lapping the entire field…Sheer class?

*30 May 1963 – Indianapolis 500 Miles. Jimmy in the Lotus-powered
by-Ford Type 29 is dwarfed by the traditional Offenhauser-engined
USAC roadsters of Jim McElreath, Eddie Sachs, Lloyd Ruby and
Roger McCluskey as he outruns them all through one of the Speedway's
shallow-banked turns. Despite being unable to close with Parnelli
Jones's leading Offy in the closing stages due to the oil it was dropping,
Jim was delighted with his second-place finish, and was quick to thank
his Indy Lotus team-mate Dan Gurney (inset) for having conceived the
idea in the first place.*

3 July 1960 – French Grand Prix, Reims-Gueux. Jim in only his third Grand Prix finished in the championship points for the second time, fifth with the Lotus 18 behind Brabham, Gendebien, McLaren and Henry Taylor – all in Coopers.

22 May 1961 – Dutch Grand Prix, Zandvoort. This extraordinary race, which saw no pit stops and no retirements, fell to 'Taffy' von Trips's 'Sharknose' Ferrari from the sister car of Phil Hill, pictured (above) leading Clark, who finished third in the latest Lotus 21, ahead of Moss and the third Ferrari of Richie Ginther. Jimmy was already living with the gods…

15 July 1962 – British Grand Prix, Aintree. Gregor Grant of
Autosport *wrote: 'What promised to be an exciting race turned into*
something of a procession, Jim Clark leading for the entire 75 laps.' As
he rewrote the record books, this would often become the case.

30 June 1963 – French Grand Prix, Reims-Gueux. Colour me gone...On a part-damp course, Jimmy won this 273-mile race at an average speed of 125.01 mph and set fastest lap at 131.15 mph driving Lotus 25 chassis R4. This was his third consecutive GP win of that championship season, and he would add four more victories for a record seven in the series.

In the office, ready to do business – in the days when crash helmets towered above roll-over bars and World Champions wore string-backed gloves, this classic Geoff Goddard shot was Motor Racing *magazine's front cover for October 1963. This schoolboy author was moved to buy a copy, wrote to the Editor for a job, and to his astonishment was offered one…Everyone's troubles start sometime. Clark was thus a major influence on mine.*

6 April 1963 – Oulton Park Spring meeting; Jim Clark won the 37-lap, 101-mile
feature race in this Normand Racing-entered Lotus 23B, with team-mate Mike
Beckwith second in the sister car after Innes Ireland's big Lotus 19 had developed
gearbox trouble.

Team Lotus 1964 and 1966 – Jim Clark, Colin Chapman and Pete Arundell. Pete was
a brilliant Formula Junior driver who shone just as brightly in his first few F1 outings
of 1964 before hurting himself badly in an F2 race at Reims. Throughout a painfully
slow recovery Colin promised him his place was secure for a comeback. Replacement
Mike Spence stood aside for Pete's return – with Clark's encouragement – in 1966, but
the old edge had gone, never to return; a tragedy.

30 August 1965 – Guards Trophy, Brands Hatch. Behold 'the Lotus 30 with ten more
mistakes' – the big 5.7-litre, 500-horsepower Ford V8-engined Type 40 which Jimmy
wrestled through one heat and a half and spun twice at South Bank before finally having
the diff seize when running a distant fifth.

1964 Indianapolis 500. Jimmy, on pole in the latest quad-cam 32-valve Lotus 34-Ford V8, Bobby Marshman in the year-old Lotus 29 and Rodger Ward's new rear-engined Watson-Offy prepare for the start. The race would be stopped almost immediately by a ghastly multiple accident, and restarted 105 minutes later. Jimmy would lead briefly before inadequate Dunlop track-race tyres would fail and vibration break his car's left-rear suspension.

1965 Indianapolis 500. Mission accomplished; Jim passed up the Monaco GP for his third attempt at the world's richest motor race, and here he is in the victorious Lotus 38-Ford V8 in which he led for 198 of the 200 laps to win at 150.686 mph, Team earning over $150,000 for the day's work. Team later took one 38 on a European exhibition tour. With a five-speed ZF gearbox fitted, Jimmy made six runs in the wet at the Swiss Ste Ursanne-Les Rangiers mountain climb – remember that, burning pure methanol, his Indy engine developed 505 bhp…

Opposite: *13 June 1965 – Belgian Grand Prix, Spa-Francorchamps.*
Four-times winner of the Ardennes classic, Clark in Lotus 33 chassis
R11 hurtles up the Raidillon hill beyond Eau Rouge.

27 June 1965 – French Grand Prix, Charade circuit, Clermont-
Ferrand. After blowing up his usual race car's engine in practice, Jimmy
drove his 'Old Faithful' Lotus 25 chassis R6 and applied his customary
race tactic of going like gangbusters from the start. His standing lap set
a new race record of 3m 23.2s and he held a two-second lead at the end of
it. He went on to lead throughout, broke the lap record another 14 times –
leaving it at 3m 18.9s – and won at record pace from Stewart's BRM.

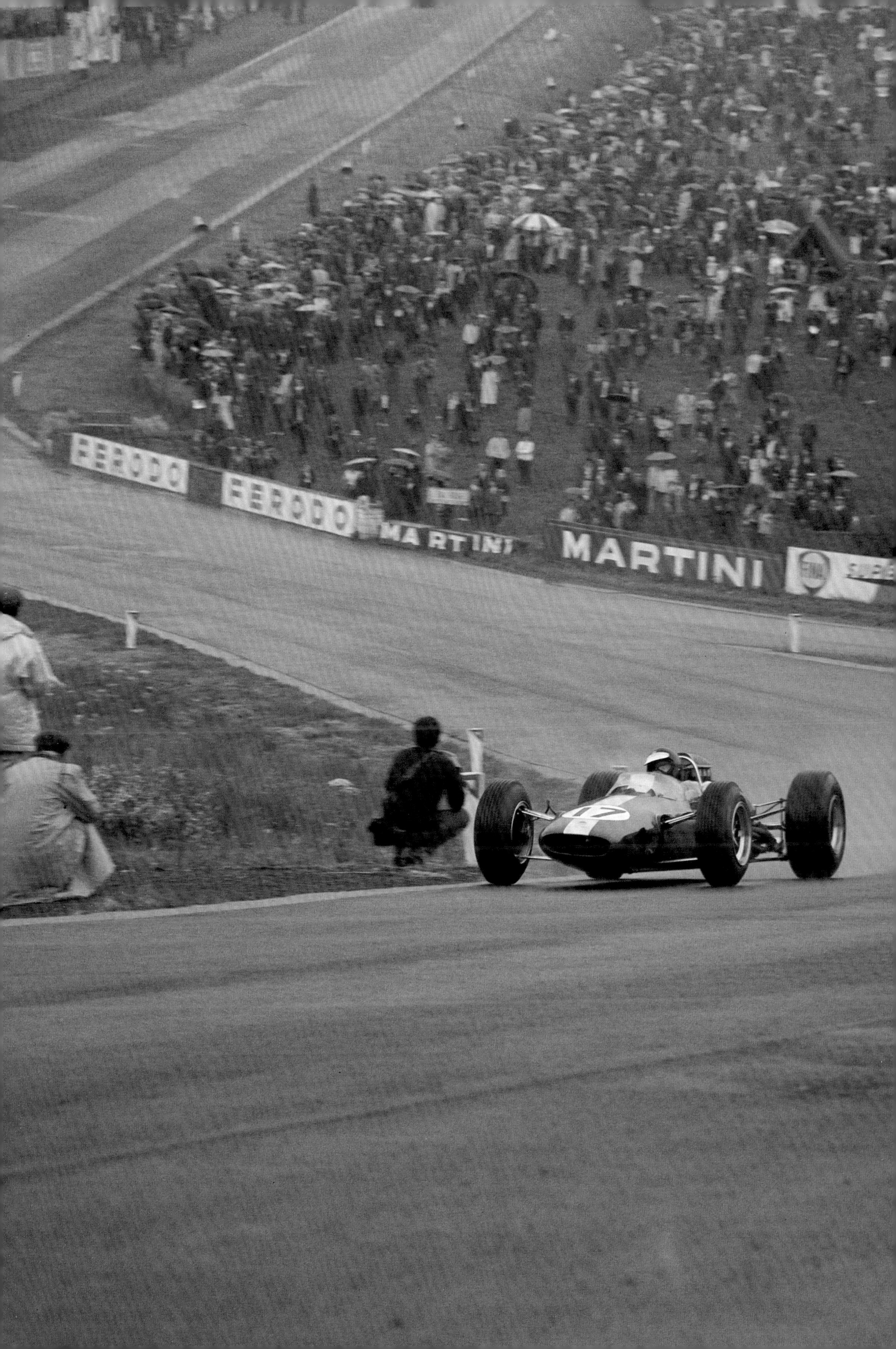
FERODO
FERODO
MARTINI
MARTINI
17

Opposite: *21 May 1966 – Monaco Grand Prix practice, Monte Carlo.*
Victory in this charismatic race was always denied to Jimmy Clark,
despite some outstanding performances there. Here in practice for the
first 3-litre formula Monaco GP he qualified his 2-litre Lotus 33 chassis
R11 on pole 0.2s quicker than John Surtees's latest 3-litre V12 Ferrari.
Jimmy's customary Monaco gremlin struck in the race as his gearbox
hung up at the start, and a rear suspension upright finally fractured to
put him out.

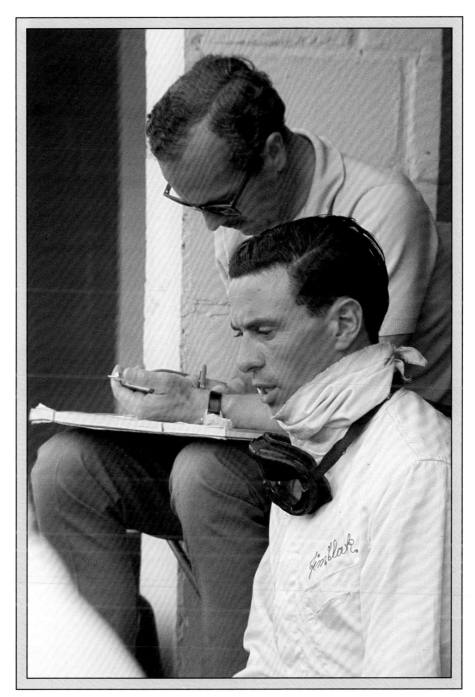

Business as usual; Chapman takes care of the science – Clark handles
the art.

Overleaf: *15 July 1967 – British Grand Prix, Silverstone. As a tax*
exile this was Jimmy's first British appearance of the 1967 season, and
he led for all but 28 mid-race laps when he played second fiddle to his
new team-mate Graham Hill in the latest Cosworth-powered Lotus
49s. It was Clark's fifth British GP victory in six years, he was
absolutely at the height of his powers, and he had started from the second
of the five pole positions he would record in the new V8 cars that year.

28 June 1964 – French Grand Prix, Rouen-les-Essarts. Clark ahead of Dan Gurney's Brabham and John Surtees's Ferrari while leading for 30 of the 57 laps – during which he lowered the circuit lap record three times – before his Climax engine holed a piston, leaving Dan to score his second Grande Épreuve victory on this same course.

11 July 1964 – British Grand Prix, Brands Hatch. Not an exciting race for most spectators but one for the real cognoscenti to savour – Jim Clark and Graham Hill fought a race-long duel, the reigning World Champion never quite able to pull away and the BRM star never quite able to close the gap. Jimmy had qualified on pole at 1m 38.1s, 0.2s quicker than Graham, he led throughout and set fastest lap at 1m 38.8s, 96.56mph, and beat Graham into second place by just 2.8 seconds – after 212 miles' relentless racing.

It was all about loyal partnership – Chapman and Clark celebrating their 1963 World Championship success in a two-up tour d'honneur on a creaking Lotus 25 at Brands Hatch (top), and then in 1965 Jimmy falling back on 'Old Faithful' Lotus 25 R6 to win the French Grand Prix at Clermont. Old R6 had begun life as Trev Taylor's 1963 car, Jimmy took it over in 1964 to win at Goodwood, Zandvoort, Spa, Brands Hatch and Enna, and now into 1965 he still used it occasionally, winning at Goodwood and here in the Auvergne.

1 August 1965 – German Grand Prix, Nürburgring. Out of this world, with his sixth GP win of the season – starting from pole position no less than 3.4 seconds faster than Jackie Stewart's second-qualifying BRM – Jimmy led all the way, set fastest lap at a record 8m 24.1s, 101.22 mph, and became World Champion Driver for the second time.

13 March 1965 – Race of Champions, Brands Hatch. Ooh – an error! Perhaps JC was human after all? After winning Heat One of this non-championship race, Jim came under heavy pressure from Dan Gurney of Brabham in Heat Two. On lap ten at Bottom Bend the Scot ran wide onto the grass verge, his Lotus 33 R10's offside wheels were trapped in a rut and even Clark's skills were unable to prevent it smashing into that earth bank. Jimmy emerged rueful yet unhurt, but the car was finished…

*24 July 1966 – Dutch Grand Prix, Zandvoort. Up against it – Jim's
2-litre Tasman Lotus-Climax versus the full 3-litre Repco V8-engined
Brabhams of 'Black Jack' himself and Denny Hulme. After an epic battle,
punctuated by a serious water leak in the Lotus's Climax engine, Jimmy
eventually finished third. It was very much the wily Brabham's year.*

*2 October 1966 – United States Grand Prix, Watkins Glen. What
Team Lotus had been waiting for all season was for BRM's full 3-litre
H16-cylinder engines to come on stream. Here with luck on his side and
BRM's own works spare H16 engine behind his shoulders, the skilled
and sensitive Clark nursed it to the only race win it would ever score.
The car is Lotus 43 R1.*

The standard-setter, now an older man – fully developed – a master craftsman at his best…

4 June 1967 – Dutch Grand Prix, Zandvoort. Over the hill and far away as Jim took over the lead from his new team-mate Graham Hill's sister Lotus-Cosworth-Ford Type 49 to win this fairy-tale debut race for the new car-and-engine combination. It was Clark's fourth Dutch GP victory in five years.

10 September 1967 – Italian Grand Prix, Monza. Jim Clark's greatest (unrewarded) drive? After starting from pole position in his regular Lotus 49 R2, Jimmy was leading the race when a tyre was punctured. He lost an entire lap while having the wheel changed in the pits and rejoined 16th. He ripped back through the field, progressively lowered the lap record, eventually equalling his pole time of 1m 28.5s, 233.898 km/h, and not only regained that whole lap but also the lead! He was narrowly ahead of Jack Brabham's BT24-Repco and John Surtees's new 'Hondola' starting the last lap, but R2 failed to pick up its last dregs of fuel – it faltered, and finally coasted across the finish line third…

1 October 1967 – United States Grand Prix, Watkins Glen. 'Lightning Tex' Hopkins displays his shy and retiring style with the chequered flag as Jim's Lotus 49 R2 yaws home to win his second consecutive (and third overall) US GP with its right-rear suspension half-collapsed. One headline read: 'The Ultimate Race Car – It Breaks at the Finish Line!' Finishing order between the Lotus drivers had been decided by the toss of a coin pre-race – Graham winning. But in the race his gearbox gave trouble and, with Chris Amon closing fast in the Ferrari, Clark whizzed by. With 13 laps to go the Ferrari broke, Graham had oil pressure worries to add to his gearbox problem, and although Jimmy cork-screwed through the final lap with that wheel adrift he still won by 6.3 seconds, at a record average speed.

Right: Clark and Chapman both enjoyed the joke, Keith Duckworth was just happy to see his new engine utterly dominant.

New Year's Day, 1968 – South African Grand Prix, Kyalami. Jimmy winning his 25th and last record-breaking World Championship GP, here leading his successor Jackie Stewart in the prototype Formula 1 Matra-DFV. His car is Lotus 49 chassis R4, Jimmy took the lead from Stewart on lap two and held it to the finish 202 miles later, he won from Graham at record speed, and he also broke the lap record three times before finally leaving it at 1m 23.7s, 109.68 mph. He would not live to start another World Championship Grand Prix, but in the two months following Kyalami he still won four more Tasman races before the end…

Above all, it had been Fun; doing what he loved doing, and what he did so well…

JIM CLARK AND USAC RACING

In 1963, when with Dan Gurney's encouragement Colin Chapman won Ford backing for an attack upon America's most prestigious and richest motor race – the Indianapolis 500 Miles – Jimmy was fascinated by the challenge. One should appreciate that he had been driving 1½-litre F1 cars and small Lotus 23 sports, so the attractions of handling a big 4.2-litre V8 single-seater were enormous. That was the main fascination; the dollar-rich prize and potential Ford bonus which were glitteringly attractive to Chapman were almost incidental to his great driver.

After that exploratory, yet epochal, first attempt in 1963 in which Jimmy's new Lotus 29 led and finished narrowly second, tyre failure ruined the '64 outing after Jimmy had again led the race in the latest Lotus 34. Qualifying his European road racing-style car fifth fastest in '63 had steadied the Establishment, and his second-place finish made them shudder – that was $55,000 denied to them! Later that year the 29s raced at Milwaukee, Jimmy qualifying on pole and leading the 200 from start to finish, lapping all but A.J. Foyt's second-placed traditional USAC roadster. In September, for the Trenton 200, Jimmy took pole with a 32-second lap, his team-mate Dan Gurney lapped in 33s and the fastest roadsters in 35s...an over-age oil-line parted to sideline Jim's car in that race.

For Indy '64, he qualified on pole, blowing off all American opposition, and Peter Warr recalls Jimmy's inability to court the intrusive US press attention which he attracted: 'His qualifying on pole really shattered the Indy establishment. There was all-day coverage of qualifying on the news media, and suddenly the foreigner had stolen the Indy pole and they all wanted to interview him, but he was rushing off to the airport to catch a flight back to Europe in time to practise for Monaco. When one of the local TV crews managed to trap him at the airport, stuck a microphone under his nose and demanded his thoughts, he stunned them by just looking distractedly up at the clock and saying, "I'm thinking if I'm going to catch my connection at Paris to get to Monaco on time..." Indy as a race was more important to them than it was to him...'

Of course Jimmy won the 500 in 1965, Peter observing: 'After the fires of 1964, pressure refuelling was banned at Indy for '65 – everybody had a standard refuelling tank delivering at a given rate. The tank had a bottom outlet which wasn't the quickest way to drain fuel because of the bath-plug effect. Colin went straight to the library to read all he could on fluid flow – he discovered a better flow method, had a new outlet welded into the side of the team's tank and selected a new type of filler hose which was smoother inside to flow faster. He also had the shut-off valve filed down to a smoother profile, but then the problem was to disguise the special hose which was a different colour to the others. We were sponsored by Enco – Esso's American brand-name – and they had their "Tiger in your Tank" advertising campaign, so the crew wrapped the hose with yellow tiger-tail tape. Cyril Audrey, the RAC timekeeper, timed a practice refill and when the chap on the shut-off valve yelled it was full they couldn't believe the time. They took the car away to check privately if it was full, and it was...Jimmy was brilliant, of course, but to some extent he won Indy in the pits...' – plus the $150,000 first

prize. Typically, he telephoned Ford executive Leo Beebe from his motel and thanked him graciously for having talked him into doing the race…

Then, qualifying in the STP-liveried 38 at Indy in '66, 'he was caught by a gust of wind and the savage motion of saving it burst open his seat-harness clip, but he didn't knock off his four-lap run, he just hurtled on with his seatbelts loose. You couldn't question his courage…'

That year Jimmy qualified his 'Granatelli Green' (dayglo orange!) 38 on the centre of the front row, as he had in '65. He led again but spun. Normally an Indy spin spells disaster, contact with the concrete wall. But Jimmy caught his car with masterly skill and raced on. Graham Hill's Lola had overtaken him during the confusion of this early spin, and he actually won by 44 seconds from the Lotus. Jimmy's confused crew had signalled him he was leading, and he headed for Victory Circle, believing he had won again. But the timekeepers located the STP crew's charting error, and second place, with its $76,992 purse, was accepted.

That October Jimmy practised the 38 for the Japanese USAC-style race at Fuji, but its engine failed in practice and the rules banned replacement so he could not start.

For 1967, as the new BRM H16 Indy engine flopped, the old 38s were prepared once again under new chief mechanic Mike Underwood. Jimmy could only qualify slower than in '66 and run 18th before the race was called off due to rain on the 18th lap. After the restart next day, Jimmy's engine grenaded, ending his last Indy 500, although he would drive a Vollstedt at Riverside, then early in '68 he would run briefly at Indy again in the prototype four-wheel drive Lotus gas turbine car. Tragically, he did not survive long enough to race it.

JIM CLARK AND LOTUS-CORTINAS

Jimmy loved racing the Lotus-Cortina saloons. It was inconsequential, wheel-waving fun. Bob Dance – who would in a later era become chief mechanic of Team Lotus – worked with Lotus Developments on cars such as the prototype twin-cam Ford-engined Lotus 23 which Jimmy drove so brilliantly to lead the Nürburgring 1000 Km in 1962. Later that year he was co-opted onto the Lotus-Cortina saloon car team. Jimmy raced the cars 22 times, normally winning his class, but it was not all easy. Bob recalls how 'Colin always liked to drive whenever we had a test day and one time at Goodwood at the end of the afternoon Colin and Jim went out together and Colin promptly spun and Jimmy rolled in avoiding him, leaving his car lying on its roof out on the track. We went round to put it back on its wheels but the shell was destroyed. We had to strip off all the useable bits and build them up on a new shell in a terrific rush because it had been Jimmy's race car and we had to get it to Snetterton for the Spring '64 meeting the following weekend.

'It was a hell of a scramble, but the rebuilt car seemed OK in practice. Then race day was wet and at the end of the warm-up lap Jimmy drove round onto the grid and I asked him, "OK?" and he said, "It's not handling right, something drastic has gone wrong." We had a look and the tracking was out by a mile, you could see the front wheels pointing in different directions.

'All we could do was to adjust it up as best we could and away he went into the race. He seemed to be going fine until at one point he suddenly slowed. He came in and said the car had been fine at the start but had become unmanageable again. We couldn't immediately see any cause but the tracking had adjusted itself out again; we couldn't figure out why, so we told him there was nothing we could do.

'In fact, during the Goodwood shunt a ball joint on the bottom of the front suspension had bent in the taper inside its rubber boot. During our rapid check of the salvaged bits it had seemed OK but the bent shank would lodge in one particular position, enabling us to track up the wheels, and then when Jimmy leaned hard on it the bent joint would suddenly click round into another position and knock the tracking out.

'But he took it all philosophically. It was all fun to him, and it was fun trying to build him a decent car because we all felt that all he needed was a reliably decent car and he would win in it for sure...

'One day Colin came in to us and said, "Would you build me that?" and it was an independent rear suspension Lotus-Cortina. Jimmy eventually took it with him up to Scotland. He really enjoyed driving the Lotus-Cortinas, he thought they were great fun and of course he was just brilliant in them...'

Up hill and down dale at Brands Hatch, or just plain on the flat at Aintree, Jim Clark and his three-wheeling works Lotus-Cortinas became a ferociously fast crowd-pleaser at British International race meetings throughout the mid-1960s...

THE GREAT DEBATE:
CLARK VERSUS STEWART

We argued about it at the time, it's argued still, and I guess it always will be when there's a gathering of students of motor racing form. Great racing drivers' careers have often overlapped; Clark's mantle was assumed by Jackie Stewart, but is it right to compare these friends, rivals and countrymen? Which of them was the greater? Indeed, is there any objective measurement by which we can tell?

Among the insiders, partiality is of course the rule. Ask Team Lotus people and there's no hesitation – 'Jimmy!' Ask BRM team members and they instantly answer – 'Jackie!'

The two Scots came from different sides of the country, from different family backgrounds, both shared enormous talent, Clark helped launch Stewart's career, both still share immense popular support. Partial fans can – and do – endlessly argue their hero's merits but I'm no believer in any truly great racing driver being measurably greater than another, except by a fan's own conviction. Various statistics can be compiled and juggled and interpreted every which way. I believe the vital factor is that Jimmy's career and his abilities had arguably reached their height by 1965–66, whereupon they perhaps reached a plateau rather than peaked.

We must not forget that Jackie Stewart did not drive his maiden F1 season until 1965, and he was still developing through '66 – the year he was undoubtedly knocked back by his heavy shunt at Spa – and '67. Neither did he have a decent 3-litre F1 car until 1968...after Jimmy's death.

But who beat whom most often? It's not that simple. The bald statistics offer no unequivocal judgement. In motor racing they simply cannot, because the vagaries of differing cars and tyres, the effects of unreliability and punctures and the occasional shunt all serve to muddy the issue. The 'Yeah but...' syndrome is a massive factor.

All I will say is that, having assessed the respective qualifying times, fastest race laps and finishes which Jimmy Clark and Jackie Stewart achieved in the 85 Formula 1, Formula 2 and Tasman events in which they raced against each other between 1964 and 1968, Jimmy got the better of Jackie 63 times to 17, with honours more or less evenly shared – by my reckoning – in their other five meetings.

Interestingly, the 33 times they faced each other in Formula 1 were resolved in Jimmy's favour 27 races to three, with three shared; their 26 meetings in Formula 2 again come down in Jimmy's favour by 17 to 7 with two shared; but their 26 Tasman clashes in 1966–67 fell markedly in Jackie's favour by a clear ratio of 19 to 7. That's where car superiority is in his favour, not perhaps vice versa as in F1 or F2...

I believe no useful purpose is served by pursuing the argument – so far as their fans are concerned, either Scot could simply walk on water. It's just that some of those fans – I will add cheerfully – are wrong...

Compatriots and chums – Clark with Helen and Jackie Stewart in the
pits, but rivals on circuit as here on 14 February 1966, starting the second
qualifying heat for the Australian Grand Prix, Warwick Farm, Sydney.
Jim is in the one-off 2½-litre Lotus-Climax 39 4-cylinder – Stewart in
the far more nimble 2-litre V8 BRM P261, and he will win.

JIM CLARK AND FORMULA TWO

30 August 1965 – British Eagle Trophy, Brands Hatch. Despite a torrid time in the 5.7-litre Lotus 40 sports in this meeting's main event, Jimmy won the 20-lap, 53-mile, 1-litre F2 race in this Ron Harris-Team Lotus 35, beating Hulme, Brabham and Hill.

It cannot be claimed that Jimmy found his feet in 1½-litre Formula 2 racing, because in effect he plunged straight into both Formula Junior and Formula 1 Lotuses in parallel in 1960, and effectively leap-frogged F2 as the intermediate step. He contested only four F2 events that year, winning one – at Brands Hatch – and qualifying once on pole position, one other time on the front row.

Of course Formula 2 lapsed from 1961 to '63, then re-emerged as a 1-litre class from 1964 to '66. Team Lotus was very active, aiming particularly at the *Grands Prix de France* Championship, 'which paid pretty well'. Jimmy contested nine of the 1964 F2 races, won four and scored three second places and a fourth in the new Type 32 monocoque cars run by Ron Harris-Team Lotus. For 1965 the improved Type 35 replaced the 32, but the opening BARC 200 at Silverstone was flooded out after Jim had qualified second fastest. However, of the following nine events he won five and added two thirds, a sixth and the usual series of pole positions, front-row places and fastest laps.

The scheduled opening race of 1966 at Oulton Park was snowed off, after Jimmy had qualified his Type 35 on pole. The handsome Lotus 44 then entered service but nothing could handle the dominant works Brabham-Hondas plus Jochen Rindt's Winkelmann Brabham-Cosworth that season, and Jimmy's nine outings yielded only a second, two thirds and a sixth.

For 1967 a new 1600 cc class took effect. The new Lotus 48 was good enough – with its Cosworth FVA engine – for Jim to win four of his 13 races, adding three thirds and a fourth, four pole positions, six other front-row starts and six fastest laps. By 1968 F2 team manager Jim Endruweit would have reason to recall the 48 as being 'not a good car', but you see when new in 1967 Jimmy was still able to make it good enough...Even in the opening round of the '68 series, at Barcelona's Montjuich Park, he had qualified second fastest, only to be punted out of the race on the second lap. His next F2 race, his 46th – he had won 14 – followed at Hockenheim on 7 April, and of course that brought it all to an end...

Above right: *5 April 1964 – Pau Grand Prix, France. The opening round of the new 1-litre Formula 2 class was a benefit for the reigning World Champion, his Lotus 32 starting from pole, leading throughout, setting fastest lap and lapping all but second-place man Richard Attwood's Lola...*

Right: *4 July 1965 – Grand Prix de Reims, France. Jim with his work cut out in the Lotus to stave off the Brabham BT 16s of Jochen Rindt and Alan Rees and Frank Gardner's Lola T60. Rindt and Gardner beat him to the line in the final slipstreaming charge, 0.3s covering all three, with Rees fourth, a further three-tenths back.*

JIM CLARK AND SPORTS CARS

Unlike Moss, or the Hills – Phil and Graham – or Surtees, Jim Clark never pursued a serious endurance racing programme. After cutting his teeth on the Border Reivers' D-Type and their famous 'flat-iron' Lister-Jaguar through 1958–59, he handled the ex-works Aston Martin DBR1/300 which Jock McBain had acquired for 1960. Jimmy raced it six times, finishing only twice, third at Oulton Park but also – excellently – at Le Mans. He loved that big, traditional, front-engined Aston and in 1961 raced it at the Nürburgring and Le Mans under the aegis of John Ogier's private but works-supported Essex Racing Stable team – then again as a Reivers entry at the end of the season in his last appearance at his old home circuit, Charterhall. He also handled 'VEV 1' – one of Ogier's two Aston Martin DB4GT Zagatos – in that year's Goodwood TT and in the Paris 1000 Km at Montlhéry.

In 1962 he drove the hefty Zagatos three more times, placing third in a supporting race at Silverstone, crashing 'VEV 2' heavily in the Goodwood TT when (on fresh tyres) he spun in the path of John Surtees's leading Ferrari 250GTO (!), and finally retiring from the Paris 1000 Km to end a rumbustious fight-back drive after an early delay. That day he made the ungainly Zagato 'go as it had never gone before'. Ogier mechanic Ian Moss remembers Jimmy as being 'Just brilliant – and such a nice feller. You can't say much more, can you...?'

Of course Jimmy gave the brand new Lotus-Ford twin-cam engine its debut in Ogier's Lotus 23 in that year's ADAC 1000 Km, as contemporary Lotus Developments mechanic – today Team's No. 1 – Bob Dance recalls: 'I took the car out there incomplete on a trailer behind a Ford van and finished building it in the paddock with Mike Costin and Ogier's mechanics. Jimmy just revelled in it and when race day was wet he simply left all the big works Ferraris for dead. He was gone. He came past the pits with about 28 seconds' lead at the end of the first lap and they just couldn't touch him until the road started to dry. Finally the exhaust broke at the 4-into-1 weld and he was affected by the fumes and finally fell off...'

That little green car with its TC head and five-bearing crank reappeared in his hands three more times that year, and in 1963 he drove the Normand team's impeccably prepared Lotus 23Bs whenever available, as team-mate to Mike Beckwith and Tony Hegbourne. Theirs was a terrific team, and Jimmy's five outings for them yielded four overall victories and one class win. He also drove a Comstock-entered 23B at Mosport in Canada, placing third in class, but he retired the Arciero Bros' elderly Lotus 19 at Laguna Seca, California that October.

Early in 1964, he made a one-off appearance in George Pitt's private Lotus 19 to win the Spring Trophy race at Oulton Park. He drove an Ian Walker 'goldbug' Elan twice, winning both times, and then in the 'dreaded' Lotus 30 with Ford V8 power – run by Ian Walker-Team Lotus – he started six of seven races entered in the unloved device, and nursed it to two first places, a second and a third – an achievement belying the car's fragile and difficult reputation.

For 1965 Lotus produced an improved Lotus 30 Series II. Jimmy raced it four times including Mosport Park, and won twice more. The 5.3-litre Lotus 40 followed, Jimmy wrestling it round Brands in the Guards Trophy until it failed him, and then finishing second in the most important Group 7 race of the year – the *Los Angeles Times* GP at Riverside, California.

And that was his last outing in a two-seat Lotus. On August Monday, 1966 he ran Peter Westbury's fascinating four-wheel drive Felday-BRM in the Guards Trophy at Brands Hatch – it broke, but only after another hugely impressive outing highlighting the car's potential when guided by the Clark touch and balance and commitment...

And thereafter it was all single-seater and saloon cars – 'til the end.

JIM CLARK · CAREER RECORD
BY JOHN TAYLOR

1956

	Race	Circuit	Date	Entrant	Car	Comment
1	Saloon Cars over 2000 cc (sprint)	Stobs Camp	03/06/56	Ecurie Agricole	Sunbeam Mk 3	only finisher
8	Sports Cars under 1200 cc	Crimond	16/06/56	Ecurie Agricole	DKW Sonderklasse	1st circuit race
1	Saloon Cars under 1200 cc (sprint)	Winfield	30/09/56	Ecurie Agricole	DKW Sonderklasse	
1	Mod. Saloons under 1500 cc (sprint)	Winfield	30/09/56	Ecurie Agricole	DKW Sonderklasse	
1	Saloons unlimited (sprint)	Winfield	30/09/56	Ecurie Agricole	Sunbeam Mk 3	
1	Mod. Saloons unlimited (sprint)	Winfield	30/09/56	Ecurie Agricole	Sunbeam Mk 3	
6	High-Speed Trial	Brunton Beadnell	07/10/56	Ecurie Agricole	DKW Sonderklasse	1st in class
6	High-Speed Trial	Brunton Beadnell	07/10/56	Ecurie Agricole	Sunbeam Mk 3	1st in class

1957

	Race	Circuit	Date	Entrant	Car	Comment
4	Prod. Car Handicap	Charterhall	30/06/57	Ecurie Agricole	DKW Sonderklasse	
8	Sports Cars 1501 cc–2700 cc	Charterhall	01/09/57	Ecurie Agricole	Sunbeam Mk 3	
3	Prod. Sports Car Handicap	Charterhall	05/10/57	Ecurie Agricole	Porsche 1600S	
2	Prod. Touring Car Handicap	Charterhall	05/10/57	Ecurie Agricole	Porsche 1600S	
1	BMRC Trophy	Charterhall	05/10/57	Ecurie Agricole	Porsche 1600S	1st circuit win
1	Mod. Saloons unlimited (sprint)	Winfield	06/10/57	Ecurie Agricole	Porsche 1600S	tie with Ian Scott-Watson
2	Sports Cars 1501 cc–3000 cc (sprint)	Winfield	06/10/57	Ecurie Agricole	Porsche 1600S	

1958

	Race	Circuit	Date	Entrant	Car	Comment
1	Racing Cars over 500 cc	Full Sutton	05/04/58	Border Reivers	Jaguar D-Type	
1	Sports Cars unlimited	Full Sutton	05/04/58	Border Reivers	Jaguar D-Type	
6	Prod. Sports Cars unlimited	Full Sutton	05/04/58	Border Reivers	Porsche 1600S	
1	Saloon Cars under 2000 cc (sprint)	Winfield	20/04/58	Border Reivers	Porsche 1600S	
2	Sports Cars unlimited	Winfield	20/04/58	Border Reivers	Porsche 1600S	
8	Formule Libre	Charterhall	27/04/58	Border Reivers	Jaguar D-Type	brake problems
4	Sports Cars 1501 cc–3000 cc	Charterhall	27/04/58	Border Reivers	Porsche 1600S	
ret	Sports Cars under 2000 cc	Charterhall	27/04/58	Border Reivers	Porsche 1600S	
8	Spa Grand Prix (over 1500 cc)	Spa	18/05/58	Border Reivers	Jaguar D-Type	1st foreign event
5	GT Specials under 2000 cc	Spa	18/05/58	Border Reivers	Porsche 1600S	
1	Sports Cars unlimited	Full Sutton	24/05/58	Border Reivers	Jaguar D-Type	
1	Formule Libre	Full Sutton	24/05/58	Border Reivers	Jaguar D-Type	
1	Saloon & GT Cars unlimited	Full Sutton	24/05/58	Border Reivers	Porsche 1600S	
1	Sports Cars under 2000 cc (sprint)	Stobs Camp	08/06/58	Border Reivers	Porsche 1600S	
2	Sports Cars under 2000 cc (sprint)	Stobs Camp	08/06/58	Border Reivers	Triumph TR3	
1	Sports Cars unlimited	Crimond	21/06/58	Border Reivers	Jaguar D-Type	
4	Sports Cars 1501 cc–3000 cc	Crimond	21/06/58	Border Reivers	Porsche 1600S	
8	Invitation Handicap	Crimond	21/06/58	Border Reivers	Jaguar D-Type	pit stop
1	Prod. Sports Cars 1501 cc–2000 cc	Rest-and-be-Thankful	28/06/58	Border Reivers	Porsche 1600S	hill climb
3	Prod. Sports Cars 1501 cc–2000 cc	Rest-and-be-Thankful	28/06/58	Border Reivers	Triumph TR3	hill climb
1	Formule Libre	Charterhall	29/06/58	Border Reivers	Jaguar D-Type	
1	Sports Cars unlimited	Charterhall	29/06/58	Border Reivers	Jaguar D-Type	
1	Sports Cars 1501 cc–2000 cc	Rest-and-be-Thankful	05/07/58	Border Reivers	Porsche 1600S	hill climb
2	Sports Cars 1501 cc–2000 cc	Rest-and-be-Thankful	05/07/58	Border Reivers	Triumph TR3	hill climb
1	Racing Cars Handicap	Charterhall	06/07/58	Border Reivers	Jaguar D-Type	
2	Touring Cars Handicap	Charterhall	06/07/58	Border Reivers	Porsche 1600S	
4	Prod. Sports Cars Handicap	Charterhall	06/07/58	Border Reivers	Porsche 1600S	
2	BMRC Trophy Handicap	Charterhall	06/07/58	Border Reivers	Jaguar D-Type	
1	Formule Libre	Full Sutton	12/07/58	Border Reivers	Jaguar D-Type	
1	Sports Cars over 1500 cc	Full Sutton	12/07/58	Border Reivers	Jaguar D-Type	
1	Prod. Sports Cars under 1600 cc	Full Sutton	12/07/58	Border Reivers	Porsche 1600S	very wet race
1	Mod. Touring Cars over 1500 cc (sprint)	Winfield	27/07/58	Border Reivers	Porsche 1600S	
1	Sports Cars 1501 cc–3000 cc (sprint)	Winfield	27/07/58	Border Reivers	Porsche 1600S	
1	Sports/Racing Cars unlimited (sprint)	Winfield	27/07/58	Border Reivers	Jaguar D-Type	
1	Sports Cars over 1500 cc	Mallory Park	04/08/58	Border Reivers	Jaguar D-Type	
2	Formule Libre–Heat	Mallory Park	04/08/58	Border Reivers	Jaguar D-Type	
7	Formule Libre–Final	Mallory Park	04/08/58	Border Reivers	Jaguar D-Type	
22	Six-Hour Relay Race (handicap)	Silverstone	16/08/58	Team Porsche	Porsche 1600S	assorted co-drivers
2	Formule Libre	Charterhall	28/09/58	Border Reivers	Jaguar D-Type	won by Ron Flockhart
3	Sports Cars over 1500 cc	Charterhall	28/09/58	Border Reivers	Jaguar D-Type	
3	Prod. Sports Cars under 1600 cc	Charterhall	28/09/58	Border Reivers	Porsche 1600S	
2	GT Cars unlimited	Brands Hatch	26/12/58	Border Reivers	Lotus Elite	won by Colin Chapman

1959

1	GT Cars 1000 cc–1600 cc	Mallory Park	30/03/59	Border Reivers	Lotus Elite	
1	Sports Cars over 1200 cc	Mallory Park	30/03/59	Border Reivers	Lister-Jaguar	
1	Formule Libre–Heat	Mallory Park	30/03/59	Border Reivers	Lister-Jaguar	
1	Formule Libre–Final	Mallory Park	30/03/59	Border Reivers	Lister-Jaguar	
10	Sports Cars under 1500 cc	Oulton Park	11/04/59	Border Reivers	Lotus Elite	
8	Sports Cars over 1500 cc	Oulton Park	11/04/59	Border Reivers	Lister-Jaguar	
6	Sports Cars over 1500 cc	Aintree	18/04/59	Border Reivers	Lister-Jaguar	
1	Sports Cars over 2000 cc	Charterhall	25/04/59	Border Reivers	Lister-Jaguar	
1	Formule Libre	Charterhall	25/04/59	Border Reivers	Lister-Jaguar	
2	GT Cars under 1600 cc	Charterhall	25/04/59	Border Reivers	Porsche 1600S	
ret	Whitsun Trophy	Goodwood	18/05/59	Border Reivers	Lister-Jaguar	out of fuel
1	Sports Cars unlimited	Rufforth	30/05/59	Border Reivers	Lister-Jaguar	
2	Formule Libre	Rufforth	30/05/59	Border Reivers	Lister-Jaguar	won by Trevor Taylor
1	GT Cars under 1600 cc (sprint)	Stobs Camp	07/06/59	Border Reivers	Porsche 1600S	
1	Sports Cars unlimited (sprint)	Stobs Camp	07/06/59	Border Reivers	Porsche 1600S	
10	Le Mans 24 Hours	Le Mans	20–21/06/59	Border Reivers	Lotus Elite	c/d John Whitmore
ret	GT World Cup Races	Zandvoort	05/07/59	Border Reivers	Lotus Elite	rear axle
1	Sports Cars over 2000 cc	Bo'ness	11/07/59	Border Reivers	Lister-Jaguar	hill climb/FTD
1	Sports Cars under 1600 cc	Bo'ness	11/07/59	Border Reivers	Lotus Elite	hill climb
7	Sports Cars under 1600 cc	Bo'ness	11/07/59	Border Reivers	Porsche 1600S	hill climb
2	Sports Cars over 2000 cc	Aintree	18/07/59	Border Reivers	Lister-Jaguar	
1	Sports Cars over 1500 cc (sprint)	Winfield	26/07/59	Border Reivers	Lister-Jaguar	
1	GT Cars 1000 cc–2000 cc (sprint)	Winfield	26/07/59	Border Reivers	Lotus Elite	
2	GT Cars 1000 cc–2000 cc (sprint)	Winfield	26/07/59	Border Reivers	Porsche 1600S	
1	Formule Libre (sprint)	Winfield	26/07/59	Border Reivers	Lister-Jaguar	FTD
3	Formule Libre–Heat	Mallory Park	02/08/59	Border Reivers	Lister-Jaguar	
4	Formule Libre–Final	Mallory Park	02/08/59	Border Reivers	Lister-Jaguar	
2	Sports Cars over 1200 cc–Heat	Mallory Park	02/08/59	Border Reivers	Lister-Jaguar	
2	Sports Cars over 1200 cc–Final	Mallory Park	02/08/59	Border Reivers	Lister-Jaguar	
2	GT Cars up to 1600 cc	Mallory Park	02/08/59	Border Reivers	Lotus Elite	pit stop–plug lead
ret	Tourist Trophy	Goodwood	18/08/59	Ecurie Ecosse	Tojeiro-Jaguar	crashed by Masten Gregory
1	GT World Cup Races–Heat 1	Brands Hatch	29/08/59	Border Reivers	Lotus Elite	
2	GT World Cup Races–Heat 2	Brands Hatch	29/08/59	Border Reivers	Lotus Elite	
1	Sports Cars over 3000 cc	Brands Hatch	29/08/59	Border Reivers	Lister-Jaguar	
1	Sports Cars over 1200 cc	Mallory Park	13/09/59	Border Reivers	Lister-Jaguar	
3	Formule Libre–Heat	Mallory Park	13/09/59	Border Reivers	Lister-Jaguar	
8	Formule Libre–Final	Mallory Park	13/09/59	Border Reivers	Lister-Jaguar	
1	GT Cars 1000 cc–1600 cc	Mallory Park	13/09/59	Border Reivers	Lotus Elite	
1	GT Cars under 1600 cc	Oulton Park	26/09/59	Border Reivers	Lotus Elite	
ret	Sports Cars over 1500 cc	Charterhall	27/09/59	Border Reivers	Lister-Jaguar	engine
5	Sports Cars under 1300 cc	Charterhall	27/09/59	Border Reivers	Lotus Elite	
1	GT Cars unlimited	Charterhall	27/09/59	Border Reivers	Lotus Elite	
1	Sports Cars over 1500 cc	Charterhall	04/10/59	Border Reivers	Lister-Jaguar	
1	Formule Libre	Charterhall	04/10/59	Border Reivers	Lister-Jaguar	
1	GT Cars unlimited	Charterhall	04/10/59	Border Reivers	Lotus Elite	
4	Sports Cars under 1300 cc	Charterhall	04/10/59	Border Reivers	Lotus Elite	
13	BMRC Trophy Handicap	Charterhall	04/10/59	Border Reivers	Lister-Jaguar	
1	Snetterton 3 Hours	Snetterton	10/10/59	Border Reivers	Lotus Elite	
ret	GT Cars unlimited	Brands Hatch	26/12/59	Border Reivers	Lotus Elite	crashed
ret	Formula Junior	Brands Hatch	26/12/59	Chequered Flag	Gemini Mk 2-Austin	flat battery

1960

1	Formula Junior	Goodwood	19/03/60	Team Lotus	FJ Lotus 18-Cosworth Ford	Fastest lap
1	Formula Junior	Oulton Park	02/04/60	Team Lotus	FJ Lotus 18-Cosworth Ford	Fastest lap
3	Sports Cars over 1100 cc	Oulton Park	02/04/60	Border Reivers	Aston Martin DBR1/300	
ret	Brussels Grand Prix–Heat 1	Heysel	10/04/60	Team Lotus	F2 Lotus 18-Climax FPF	engine
1	Formula Junior	Goodwood	16/04/60	Team Lotus	FJ Lotus 18-Cosworth Ford	Fastest lap
ret	Sports Cars unlimited	Goodwood	16/04/60	Border Reivers	Aston Martin DBR1/300	fuel starvation
9	Aintree 200	Aintree	30/04/60	Team Lotus	F2 Lotus 18-Climax FPF	Ireland took over
ret	Formula Junior	Aintree	30/04/60	Team Lotus	FJ Lotus 18-Cosworth Ford	crashed/Fastest lap
1	Formula Junior	Silverstone	14/05/60	Team Lotus	FJ Lotus 18-Cosworth Ford	
ret	Sports Cars unlimited	Silverstone	14/05/60	Border Reivers	Aston Martin DBR1/300	throttle linkage
ret	Nürburgring 1000 Km	Nürburgring	22/05/60	Border Reivers	Aston Martin DBR1/300	engine/c/d Roy Salvadori
7	Formula Junior	Monte Carlo	27/05/60	Team Lotus	FJ Lotus 18-Cosworth Ford	ignition/Pole/Fastest lap
ret	**DUTCH GP**	Zandvoort	05/06/60	Team Lotus	F1 Lotus 18-Climax FPF	gearbox
5	**BELGIAN GP**	Spa	19/06/60	Team Lotus	F1 Lotus 18-Climax FPF	
3	Le Mans 24 Hours	Le Mans	25–26/06/60	Border Reivers	Aston Martin DBR1/300	c/d Roy Salvadori
5	**FRENCH GP**	Reims	03/07/60	Team Lotus	F1 Lotus 18-Climax FPF	
16	**BRITISH GP**	Silverstone	16/07/60	Team Lotus	F1 Lotus 18-Climax FPF	pit stop–suspension
8	Solitude Grand Prix	Solitude	24/07/60	Team Lotus	F2 Lotus 18-Climax FPF	pit stop–water/Pole

1960 (continued)

Pos	Event	Circuit	Date	Entrant	Car	Notes
1	Formula Junior	Solitude	24/07/60	Team Lotus	FJ Lotus 18-Cosworth Ford	*Fastest lap*
ret	Silver City Trophy	Brands Hatch	01/08/60	Team Lotus	F1 Lotus 18-Climax FPF	*transmission/Pole/Fastest lap*
1	Formula Junior	Brands Hatch	01/08/60	Team Lotus	FJ Lotus 18-Cosworth Ford	*Pole/Fastest lap*
3	**PORTUGUESE GP**	Oporto	14/08/60	Team Lotus	F1 Lotus 18-Climax FPF	
1	BARC FJ Championship–Heat 2	Goodwood	19/08/60	Team Lotus	FJ Lotus 18-Cosworth Ford	*Fastest lap*
2	BARC FJ Championship–Final	Goodwood	19/08/60	Team Lotus	FJ Lotus 18-Cosworth Ford	*won by Trevor Taylor*
1	Kentish 100	Brands Hatch	27/08/60	Team Lotus	F2 Lotus 18-Climax FPF	
2	Formula Junior	Brands Hatch	27/08/60	Team Lotus	FJ Lotus 18-Cosworth Ford	*spin*
2	Lombank Trophy	Snetterton	17/09/60	Team Lotus	F1 Lotus 18-Climax FPF	*Fastest lap*
2	Formula Junior	Snetterton	17/09/60	Team Lotus	FJ Lotus 18-Cosworth Ford	
ret	Gold Cup	Oulton Park	24/09/60	Team Lotus	F1 Lotus 18-Climax FPF	*collision Naylor/Fastest lap*
1	Formula Junior–Heat 1	Oulton Park	24/09/60	Team Lotus	FJ Lotus 18-Cosworth Ford	*Pole*
1	Formula Junior–Heat 2	Oulton Park	24/09/60	Team Lotus	FJ Lotus 18-Cosworth Ford	*Pole*
1	Formula Junior–Aggregate	Oulton Park	24/09/60	Team Lotus	FJ Lotus 18-Cosworth Ford	
ret	*Formule Libre*	Charterhall	25/09/60	Team Lotus	FJ Lotus 18-Cosworth Ford	*transmission*
ret	Paris 1000 Km	Montlhéry	31/10/60	Essex Racing Team	Aston Martin DBR1/300	*engine/c/d Tony Maggs*
16	**US GP**	Riverside	20/11/60	Team Lotus	F1 Lotus 18-Climax FPF	*collision with Surtees*
1	Formula Junior	Brands Hatch	26/12/60	Team Lotus	FJ Lotus 18-Cosworth Ford	*Fastest lap*

1961

Pos	Event	Circuit	Date	Entrant	Car	Notes
7	New Zealand Grand Prix	Ardmore	07/01/61	Team Lotus	F Int. Lotus 18-Climax FPF	
2	Vic Hudson Trophy	Levin	14/01/61	Team Lotus	F Int. Lotus 18-Climax FPF	
ret	Lady Wigram Trophy	Christchurch	21/01/61	Team Lotus	F Int. Lotus 18-Climax FPF	*spun off/Pole*
6	Lombank Trophy	Snetterton	26/03/61	Team Lotus	F1 Lotus 18-Climax FPF	*4th in F1 class*
1	Pau Grand Prix	Pau	03/04/61	Team Lotus	F1 Lotus 18-Climax FPF	*Fastest lap*
ret	Brussels Grand Prix–Heat 1	Heysel	09/04/61	Team Lotus	F1 Lotus 18-Climax FPF	*gearbox*
9	Aintree 200	Aintree	22/04/61	Team Lotus	F1 Lotus 18-Climax FPF	
6	Syracuse Grand Prix	Syracuse	25/04/61	Team Lotus	F1 Lotus 18-Climax FPF	
8	International Trophy	Silverstone	06/05/61	Team Lotus	F Int. Lotus 18-Climax FPF	
10	**MONACO GP**	Monte Carlo	14/05/61	Team Lotus	F1 Lotus 21-Climax FPF	*pit stop–ignition*
3	**DUTCH GP**	Zandvoort	22/05/61	Team Lotus	F1 Lotus 21-Climax FPF	*Fastest lap*
ret	Nürburgring 1000 Km	Nürburgring	28/05/61	Essex Racing Team	Aston Martin DBR1/300	*engine/c/d Bruce McLaren*
2	Silver City Trophy	Brands Hatch	03/06/61	Team Lotus	F1 Lotus 21-Climax FPF	
ret	Le Mans 24 Hours	Le Mans	09–10/06/61	Essex Racing Team	Aston Martin DBR1/300	*clutch/c/d Ron Flockhart*
12	**BELGIAN GP**	Spa	18/06/61	Team Lotus	F1 Lotus 21-Climax FPF	*pit stop*
3	**FRENCH GP**	Reims	02/07/61	Team Lotus	F1 Lotus 21-Climax FPF	
5	British Empire Trophy	Silverstone	09/07/61	Team Lotus	F Int. Lotus 18-Climax FPF	
ret	**BRITISH GP**	Aintree	15/07/61	Team Lotus	F1 Lotus 21-Climax FPF	*oil pipe*
7	Solitude Grand Prix	Solitude	23/07/61	Team Lotus	F1 Lotus 21-Climax FPF	
4	**GERMAN GP**	Nürburgring	06/08/61	Team Lotus	F1 Lotus 21-Climax FPF	
2	Guards Trophy	Brands Hatch	07/08/61	Team Lotus	F Int. Lotus 18-Climax FPF	
4	Tourist Trophy	Goodwood	19/08/61	Essex Racing Team	Aston Martin DB4GT Zagato	
ret	Kanonloppet	Karlskoga	20/08/61	Team Lotus	F1 Lotus 21-Climax FPF	*Pole*
6	Danish Grand Prix–Heat 1	Roskildering	26/08/61	Team Lotus	F1 Lotus 18-Climax FPF	
ret	Danish Grand Prix–Heat 2	Roskildering	27/08/61	Team Lotus	F1 Lotus 18-Climax FPF	*steering*
4	Danish Grand Prix–Heat 3	Roskildering	27/08/61	Team Lotus	F1 Lotus 18-Climax FPF	
7	Danish Grand Prix–Aggregate	Roskildering	26–27/08/61	Team Lotus	F1 Lotus 18-Climax FPF	
4	Modena Grand Prix	Modena	03/09/61	Team Lotus	F1 Lotus 21-Climax FPF	
ret	**ITALIAN GP**	Monza	10/09/61	Team Lotus	F1 Lotus 21-Climax FPF	*collision with von Trips*
4	Flugplatzrennen	Zeltweg	17/09/61	Team Lotus	F1 Lotus 21-Climax FPF	
ret	Gold Cup	Oulton Park	23/09/61	Team Lotus	F1 Lotus 21-Climax FPF	
2	*Formule Libre*	Charterhall	24/09/61	Border Reivers	Aston Martin DBR1/300	
2	Sports Cars unlimited	Charterhall	24/09/61	Border Reivers	Aston Martin DBR1/300	
7	**US GP**	Watkins Glen	08/10/61	Team Lotus	F1 Lotus 21-Climax FPF	*slipping clutch*
6	Paris 1000 Km	Montlhéry	15/10/61	Essex Racing Team	Aston Martin DB4GT Zagato	*c/d Innes Ireland*
1	Rand Grand Prix	Kyalami	09/12/61	Team Lotus	F1 Lotus 21-Climax FPF	*Pole*
1	Natal Grand Prix	Westmead	17/12/61	Team Lotus	F1 Lotus 21-Climax FPF	*Pole*
1	South African Grand Prix	East London	26/12/61	Team Lotus	F1 Lotus 21-Climax FPF	*Pole/Fastest lap*

1962

Pos	Event	Circuit	Date	Entrant	Car	Notes
2	Cape Grand Prix	Killarney	02/01/62	Team Lotus	F1 Lotus 21-Climax FPF	*Pole/Fastest lap*
4 cl	Daytona Intercontinental GT	Daytona	11/03/62	Peter Berry	Lotus Elite	*battery problems*
2	Sandown Park International–Heat	Sandown Park	12/03/62	Team Lotus	F Int. Lotus 21-Climax FPF	
6	Sandown Park International–Final	Sandown Park	12/03/62	Team Lotus	F Int. Lotus 21-Climax FPF	
ret	Brussels Grand Prix–Heat 1	Heysel	01/04/62	Team Lotus	F1 Lotus 24-Climax FWMV	*engine*
1	Lombank Trophy	Snetterton	14/04/62	Team Lotus	F1 Lotus 24-Climax FWMV	
ret	Pau Grand Prix	Pau	23/04/62	Team Lotus	F1 Lotus 24-Climax FWMV	*gear linkage/Pole/Fastest lap*
1	Aintree 200	Aintree	28/04/62	Team Lotus	F1 Lotus 24-Climax FWMV	*Pole/Fastest lap*
2	International Trophy	Silverstone	12/05/62	Team Lotus	F1 Lotus 24-Climax FWMV	*Fastest lap*
3	GT Cars unlimited	Silverstone	12/05/62	Essex Racing Team	Aston Martin DB4GT Zagato	

1962 (continued)

9	**DUTCH GP**	Zandvoort	20/05/62	Team Lotus	F1 Lotus 25-Climax FWMV	*pit stop–gearbox*
ret	Nürburgring 1000 Km	Nürburgring	27/05/62	Essex Racing Team	Lotus 23-Lotus Ford T/C	*exhaust leak–accident*
ret	**MONACO GP**	Monte Carlo	03/06/62	Team Lotus	F1 Lotus 25-Climax FWMV	*clutch/Pole/Fastest lap*
ret	International 2000 Guineas	Mallory Park	11/06/62	Team Lotus	F1 Lotus 25-Climax FWMV	*oil pressure/Pole*
1	**BELGIAN GP**	Spa	17/06/62	Team Lotus	F1 Lotus 25-Climax FWMV	*Fastest lap*
ret	Reims Grand Prix	Reims	01/07/62	Team Lotus	F1 Lotus 25-Climax FWMV	*header tank/Pole*
ret	Reims Grand Prix	Reims	01/07/62	Team Lotus	F1 Lotus 24-BRM	*out of fuel/Arundell's car*
ret	**FRENCH GP**	Rouen	08/07/62	Team Lotus	F1 Lotus 25-Climax FWMV	*suspension/Pole*
ret	Solitude Grand Prix	Solitude	15/07/62	Team Lotus	F1 Lotus 25-Climax FWMV	*accident/Pole*
1	**BRITISH GP**	Aintree	21/07/62	Team Lotus	F1 Lotus 25-Climax FWMV	*Pole/Fastest lap*
4	**GERMAN GP**	Nürburgring	05/08/62	Team Lotus	F1 Lotus 25-Climax FWMV	*stalled on grid*
ret	Guards Trophy	Brands Hatch	06/08/62	Essex Racing Team	Lotus 23-Lotus Ford T/C	*clutch*
ret	Tourist Trophy	Goodwood	18/08/62	Essex Racing Team	Aston Martin DB4GT Zagato	*crashed*
nc	Swiss Mountain Grand Prix	Ollon-Villars	26/08/62	Scuderia Filipinetti	F1 Lotus 21-Climax FPF	*hill climb*
2	Sports Cars up to 1600 cc	Oulton Park	01/09/62	Essex Racing Team	Lotus 23-Lotus Ford T/C	
1	Gold Cup	Oulton Park	01/09/62	Team Lotus	F1 Lotus 25-Climax FWMV	*Fastest lap*
ret	**ITALIAN GP**	Monza	16/09/62	Team Lotus	F1 Lotus 25-Climax FWMV	*gearbox/Pole*
dsq	*Autosport* 3 Hours	Snetterton	29/09/62	Essex Racing Team	Lotus 23-Lotus Ford T/C	*push-start*
1	**US GP**	Watkins Glen	07/10/62	Team Lotus	F1 Lotus 25-Climax FWMV	*Pole/Fastest lap*
ret	Paris 1000 Km	Montlhéry	21/10/62	Essex Racing Team	Aston Martin DB4GT Zagato	*engine/c/d John Whitmore*
dsq	Mexican Grand Prix	Mexico City	04/11/62	Team Lotus	F1 Lotus 25-Climax FWMV	*push-start/Pole*
1	Mexican Grand Prix	Mexico City	04/11/62	Team Lotus	F1 Lotus 25-Climax FWMV	*T. Taylor's car/Fastest lap*
1	Rand Grand Prix	Kyalami	15/12/62	Team Lotus	F1 Lotus 25-Climax FWMV	*Pole/Fastest lap*
12	Natal Grand Prix–Heat 1	Westmead	22/12/62	Team Lotus	F1 Lotus 25-Climax FWMV	*pit stop/Pole*
2	Natal Grand Prix–Final	Westmead	22/12/62	Team Lotus	F1 Lotus 25-Climax FWMV	
ret	**SOUTH AFRICAN GP**	East London	29/12/62	Team Lotus	F1 Lotus 25-Climax FWMV	*oil leak/Pole/Fastest lap*

1963

2	Lombank Trophy	Snetterton	30/03/63	Team Lotus	F1 Lotus 25-Climax FWMV	*Pole*
1	British Empire Trophy	Oulton Park	06/04/63	Normand Racing	Lotus 23B-Lotus Ford T/C	
1	Pau Grand Prix	Pau	15/04/63	Team Lotus	F1 Lotus 25-Climax FWMV	*Pole/Fastest lap*
1	Imola Grand Prix	Imola	21/04/63	Team Lotus	F1 Lotus 25-Climax FWMV	*Pole*
7	Aintree 200	Aintree	27/04/63	Team Lotus	F1 Lotus 25-Climax FWMV	*Trevor Taylor took over/Pole*
3	Aintree 200	Aintree	27/04/63	Team Lotus	F1 Lotus 25-Climax FWMV	*Taylor's car/Fastest lap*
1	International Trophy	Silverstone	11/05/63	Team Lotus	F1 Lotus 25-Climax FWMV	
8/*ret*	**MONACO GP**	Monte Carlo	26/05/63	Team Lotus	F1 Lotus 25-Climax FWMV	*gearbox/Pole*
2	Indianapolis 500	Indianapolis	30/05/63	Team Lotus	USAC Lotus 29-Ford AX320-2	*won by Parnelli Jones*
8	Player's 200	Mosport Park	01/06/63	Comstock Racing	Lotus 23B-Lotus Ford T/C	*3rd in class*
1	Sports Cars unlimited	Crystal Palace	03/06/63	Normand Racing	Lotus 23B-Lotus Ford T/C	
1	**BELGIAN GP**	Spa	09/06/63	Team Lotus	F1 Lotus 25-Climax FWMV	*Fastest lap*
1	**DUTCH GP**	Zandvoort	23/06/63	Team Lotus	F1 Lotus 25-Climax FWMV	*Pole/Fastest lap*
1	**FRENCH GP**	Reims	30/06/63	Team Lotus	F1 Lotus 25-Climax FWMV	*Pole/Fastest lap*
1	**BRITISH GP**	Silverstone	20/07/63	Team Lotus	F1 Lotus 25-Climax FWMV	*Pole*
nc	Solitude Grand Prix	Solitude	28/07/63	Team Lotus	F1 Lotus 25-Climax FWMV	*late away/Pole/Fastest lap*
2	**GERMAN GP**	Nürburgring	04/08/63	Team Lotus	F1 Lotus 25-Climax FWMV	*Pole*
1	Slip Molyslip Trophy	Brands Hatch	05/08/63	Alan Brown	Ford Galaxie	
1	Kanonloppet–Heat 1	Karlskoga	11/08/63	Team Lotus	F1 Lotus 25-Climax FWMV	*Fastest lap*
3	Kanonloppet–Heat 2	Karlskoga	11/08/63	Team Lotus	F1 Lotus 25-Climax FWMV	*Pole*
1	Kanonloppet–Aggregate	Karlskoga	11/08/63	Team Lotus	F1 Lotus 25-Climax FWMV	
1	Milwaukee 200	Milwaukee	18/08/63	Team Lotus	USAC Lotus 29-Ford AX320-2	*Pole*
ret	Austrian Grand Prix	Zeltweg	01/09/63	Team Lotus	F1 Lotus 25-Climax FWMV	*oil pipe/Pole*
1	**ITALIAN GP**	Monza	08/09/63	Team Lotus	F1 Lotus 25-Climax FWMV	*Fastest lap*
1	Gold Cup	Oulton Park	21/09/63	Team Lotus	F1 Lotus 25-Climax FWMV	*Pole/Fastest lap*
1	Sports Cars up to 2000 cc	Oulton Park	21/09/63	Normand Racing	Lotus 23B-Lotus Ford T/C	
ret	Trenton 200	Trenton	22/09/63	Team Lotus	USAC Lotus 29-Ford AX320-2	*oil leak/Pole*
1	Snetterton 3 Hours	Snetterton	28/09/63	Normand Racing	Lotus 23B-Lotus Ford T/C	
2	Saloon Cars unlimited	Snetterton	28/09/63	Team Lotus	Lotus-Cortina	*1st in class/class Fastest lap*
3	**US GP**	Watkins Glen	06/10/63	Team Lotus	F1 Lotus 25-Climax FWMV	*stalled on grid/Fastest lap*
5	Riverside Grand Prix	Riverside	13/10/63	Frank Arciero	Lotus 23B-Lotus Ford T/C	*1st in class*
ret	Pacific Grand Prix	Laguna Seca	20/10/63	Frank Arciero	Lotus 19-Climax FPF	*engine*
1	**MEXICAN GP**	Mexico City	27/10/63	Team Lotus	F1 Lotus 25-Climax FWMV	*Pole/Fastest lap*
19	Rand Grand Prix–Heat 1	Kyalami	14/12/63	Team Lotus	F1 Lotus 25-Climax FWMV	*fuel pump problems*
5	Rand Grand Prix–Heat 2	Kyalami	14/12/63	Team Lotus	F1 Lotus 25-Climax FWMV	
16	Rand Grand Prix–Aggregate	Kyalami	14/12/63	Team Lotus	F1 Lotus 25-Climax FWMV	
1	**SOUTH AFRICAN GP**	East London	28/12/63	Team Lotus	F1 Lotus 25-Climax FWMV	*Pole*

1964

Pos	Event	Circuit	Date	Entrant	Car	Notes
ret	*Daily Mirror* Trophy	Snetterton	14/03/64	Team Lotus	F1 Lotus 25-Climax FWMV	*ignition/Pole*
2	Saloon Cars unlimited	Snetterton	14/03/64	Team Lotus	Lotus-Cortina	*1st in class*
3	Saloon Cars unlimited	Sebring	22/03/64	Team Lotus	Lotus-Cortina	*1st in class*
21	Sebring 12 Hours	Sebring	23/03/64	Team Lotus	Lotus-Cortina	*2nd in class/c/d Hay Parsons*
1	*News of the World* Trophy	Goodwood	30/03/64	Team Lotus	F1 Lotus 25-Climax FWMV	
2	Saloon Cars unlimited	Goodwood	30/03/64	Team Lotus	Lotus-Cortina	*1st in class/class Fastest lap*
1	Pau Grand Prix	Pau	05/04/64	Ron Harris-Team Lotus	F2 Lotus 32-Cosworth SCA	*Pole/Fastest lap*
1	Saloon Cars unlimited	Oulton Park	11/04/64	Team Lotus	Lotus-Cortina	*Fastest lap*
1	Sports Cars unlimited	Oulton Park	11/04/64	George Pitt	Lotus 19-Climax FPF	*Fastest lap*
1	GT Cars up to 2500 cc	Oulton Park	11/04/64	Ian Walker-Team Lotus	Lotus Elan	*Fastest lap*
ret	Aintree 200	Aintree	18/04/64	Team Lotus	F1 Lotus 25-Climax FWMV	*accident/Fastest lap*
2	Sports Cars unlimited	Aintree	18/04/64	Ian Walker-Team Lotus	Lotus 30-Ford	*1st in class/Fastest lap*
3	Saloon Cars unlimited	Aintree	18/04/64	Team Lotus	Lotus-Cortina	*1st in class/class Fastest lap*
1	Eifelrennen	Nürburgring	26/04/64	Ron Harris-Team Lotus	F2 Lotus 32-Cosworth SCA	*Pole/Fastest lap*
ret	*Daily Express* International Trophy	Silverstone	02/05/64	Team Lotus	F1 Lotus 25-Climax FWMV	
10	GT cars unlimited	Silverstone	02/05/64	Ian Walker-Team Lotus	Lotus Elan	*1st in class/class Fastest lap*
dns	Sports cars unlimited	Silverstone	02/05/64	Ian Walker-Team Lotus	Lotus 30-Ford	*fuel injection*
3	Saloon Cars unlimited	Silverstone	02/05/64	Team Lotus	Lotus-Cortina	*1st in class/class Fastest lap*
4/ret	**MONACO GP**	Monte Carlo	10/05/64	Team Lotus	F1 Lotus 25-Climax FWMV	*engine/Pole*
1	Grovewood Trophy	Mallory Park	16/05/64	Ron Harris-Team Lotus	F2 Lotus 32-Cosworth SCA	*Fastest lap*
1	Sports Cars over 2000 cc	Mallory Park	16/05/64	Ian Walker-Team Lotus	Lotus 30-Ford	*Pole/Fastest lap*
2	London Trophy–Heat 1	Crystal Palace	18/05/64	Ron Harris-Team Lotus	F2 Lotus 32-Cosworth SCA	
10	London Trophy–Final	Crystal Palace	18/05/64	Ron Harris-Team Lotus	F2 Lotus 32-Cosworth SCA	*pit stop/plug lead*
1	Saloon Cars over 1300 cc	Crystal Palace	18/05/64	Team Lotus	Lotus-Cortina	
1	**DUTCH GP**	Zandvoort	24/05/64	Team Lotus	F1 Lotus 25-Climax FWMV	*Fastest lap*
ret	Indianapolis 500	Indianapolis	30/05/64	Team Lotus	USAC Lotus 34-Ford 4-cam	*suspension/Pole*
1	**BELGIAN GP**	Spa	14/06/64	Team Lotus	F1 Lotus 25-Climax FWMV	
ret	**FRENCH GP**	Rouen	28/06/64	Team Lotus	F1 Lotus 25-Climax FWMV	*engine/Pole*
4	Reims Grand Prix	Reims	05/07/64	Ron Harris-Team Lotus	F2 Lotus 32-Cosworth SCA	
1	**BRITISH GP**	Brands Hatch	11/07/64	Team Lotus	F1 Lotus 25-Climax FWMV	*Pole/Fastest lap*
1	Solitude Grand Prix	Solitude	19/07/64	Team Lotus	F1 Lotus 25-Climax FWMV	*Pole/Fastest lap*
ret	**GERMAN GP**	Nürburgring	02/08/64	Team Lotus	F1 Lotus 25-Climax FWMV	*engine*
1	British Eagle Trophy	Brands Hatch	03/08/64	Ron Harris-Team Lotus	F2 Lotus 32-Cosworth SCA	
ret	Guards Trophy	Brands Hatch	03/08/64	Ian Walker-Team Lotus	Lotus 30-Ford	*fuel pump on grid*
2	Saloon Cars unlimited	Brands Hatch	03/08/64	Team Lotus	Lotus-Cortina	*1st in class*
1	Kanonloppet–Heat 1	Karlskoga	09/08/64	Ron Harris-Team Lotus	F2 Lotus 32-Cosworth SCA	*Pole*
2	Kanonloppet–Final	Karlskoga	09/08/64	Ron Harris-Team Lotus	F2 Lotus 32-Cosworth SCA	*Pole*
2	Mediterranean Grand Prix	Enna	16/08/64	Team Lotus	F1 Lotus 25-Climax FWMV	
ret	**AUSTRIAN GP**	Zeltweg	23/08/64	Team Lotus	F1 Lotus 33-Climax FWMV	*driveshaft*
12	Tourist Trophy	Goodwood	29/08/64	Ian Walker-Team Lotus	Lotus 30-Ford	*pit stop–suspension*
ret	**ITALIAN GP**	Monza	06/09/64	Team Lotus	F1 Lotus 33-Climax FWMV	*engine*
ret	Albi Grand Prix	Albi	13/09/64	Ron Harris-Team Lotus	F2 Lotus 32-Cosworth SCA	*engine*
2	Gold Cup	Oulton Park	19/09/64	Ron Harris-Team Lotus	F2 Lotus 32-Cosworth SCA	*Fastest lap*
1	Saloon Cars unlimited	Oulton Park	19/09/64	Team Lotus	Lotus-Cortina	*Fastest lap*
ret	Canadian Grand Prix	Mosport Park	26/09/64	Ian Walker-Team Lotus	Lotus 30-Ford	*accident damage*
ret	Trenton 200	Trenton	27/09/64	Team Lotus	USAC Lotus 34-Ford 4-cam	*engine*
ret	**US GP**	Watkins Glen	04/10/64	Team Lotus	F1 Lotus 25-Climax FWMV	*engine/Spence took over/Pole*
7/ret	**US GP**	Watkins Glen	04/10/64	Team Lotus	F1 Lotus 33-Climax FWMV	*fuel/Spence's car/Fastest lap*
3	*Times* Grand Prix	Riverside	11/10/64	Ian Walker-Team Lotus	Lotus 30-Ford	
5/ret	**MEXICAN GP**	Mexico City	25/10/64	Team Lotus	F1 Lotus 33-Climax FWMV	*engine/Pole/Fastest lap*

31 May 1964 – Indianapolis 500 Miles. The Lotus 34 subsides on the inside verge after vibration from Dunlop's chunking tyre had broken its suspension. As Jimmy walked to the pits a bystander exclaimed how shocked he had been at the sight; Clark replied, 'You should have been where I was, mate...'

1965

1	**SOUTH AFRICAN GP**	East London	01/01/65	Team Lotus	F1 Lotus 33-Climax FWMV	*Pole/Fastest lap*
1	New Zealand Grand Prix–Preliminary	Pukekohe	10/01/65	Team Lotus	FT Lotus 32B-Climax FPF	
ret	New Zealand Grand Prix	Pukekohe	10/01/65	Team Lotus	FT Lotus 32B-Climax FPF	*hit by McLaren*
1	Gold Leaf Trophy–Preliminary	Levin	16/01/65	Team Lotus	FT Lotus 32B-Climax FPF	*Pole/Fastest lap*
1	Gold Leaf Trophy	Levin	16/01/65	Team Lotus	FT Lotus 32B-Climax FPF	*Pole/Fastest lap*
1	Flying Farewell	Levin	16/01/65	Team Lotus	FT Lotus 32B-Climax FPF	*Pole/Fastest lap*
1	Lady Wigram Trophy–Heat 2	Christchurch	23/01/65	Team Lotus	FT Lotus 32B-Climax FPF	*Pole*
1	Lady Wigram Trophy–Final	Christchurch	23/01/65	Team Lotus	FT Lotus 32B-Climax FPF	*Pole*
1	Teretonga Trophy–Heat 1	Invercargill	30/01/65	Team Lotus	FT Lotus 32B-Climax FPF	*Pole/Fastest lap*
1	Teretonga Trophy–Final	Invercargill	30/01/65	Team Lotus	FT Lotus 32B-Climax FPF	*Pole/Fastest lap*
2	Flying Farewell	Invercargill	30/01/65	Team Lotus	FT Lotus 32B-Climax FPF	*Pole*
1	Warwick Farm 100	Warwick Farm	14/02/65	Team Lotus	FT Lotus 32B-Climax FPF	*Fastest lap*
2	International Cup	Sandown Park	21/02/65	Team Lotus	FT Lotus 32B-Climax FPF	
7	*Launceston Examiner* Trophy	Longford	01/03/65	Team Lotus	FT Lotus 32B-Climax FPF	
5	Australian Grand Prix	Longford	03/03/65	Team Lotus	FT Lotus 32B-Climax FPF	
1	Lakeside 99	Lakeside	07/03/65	Team Lotus	FT Lotus 32B-Climax FPF	*Pole/Fastest lap*
1	Race of Champions–Heat 1	Brands Hatch	13/03/65	Team Lotus	F1 Lotus 33-Climax FWMV	*Pole/Fastest lap*
ret	Race of Champions–Heat 2	Brands Hatch	13/03/65	Team Lotus	F1 Lotus 33-Climax FWMV	*crashed/Pole/Fastest lap*
ret	Race of Champions–Aggregate	Brands Hatch	13/03/65	Team Lotus	F1 Lotus 33-Climax FWMV	*crashed/Fastest lap*
ret	Saloon Cars unlimited	Brands Hatch	13/03/65	Team Lotus	Lotus-Cortina	*lost wheel/Fastest lap*
1	Guards Trophy	Silverstone	20/03/65	Ian Walker-Team Lotus	Lotus 30-Ford	*Pole/Fastest lap*
1	Sebring 3 Hours	Sebring	26/03/65	Team Lotus	Lotus-Cortina	*Pole/Fastest lap*
1	Syracuse Grand Prix	Syracuse	04/04/65	Team Lotus	F1 Lotus 33-Climax FWMV	*Pole/Fastest lap*
2	*Autocar* Trophy–Heat 1	Snetterton	10/04/65	Ron Harris-Team Lotus	F2 Lotus 32-Cosworth SCA	*Fastest lap*
6	*Autocar* Trophy–Heat 2	Snetterton	10/04/65	Ron Harris-Team Lotus	F2 Lotus 32-Cosworth SCA	*low oil pressure*
3	*Autocar* Trophy–Aggregate	Snetterton	10/04/65	Ron Harris-Team Lotus	F2 Lotus 32-Cosworth SCA	
5	Saloon Cars unlimited	Snetterton	10/04/65	Team Lotus	Lotus-Cortina	*2nd in class*
1	*Sunday Mirror* Trophy	Goodwood	19/04/65	Team Lotus	F1 Lotus 33-Climax FWMV	*Fastest lap*
1	Lavant Cup–Sports Cars unlimited	Goodwood	19/04/65	Ian Walker-Team Lotus	Lotus 30-Ford	*Fastest lap*
1	Saloon Cars unlimited	Goodwood	19/04/65	Team Lotus	Lotus-Cortina	*Fastest lap*
1	Pau Grand Prix	Pau	25/04/65	Ron Harris-Team Lotus	F2 Lotus 35-Cosworth SCA	
16	Tourist Trophy–Heat 1	Oulton Park	01/05/65	Ian Walker-Team Lotus	Lotus 30-Ford	*stop–suspension/Fastest lap*
ret	Tourist Trophy–Heat 2	Oulton Park	01/05/65	Ian Walker-Team Lotus	Lotus 30-Ford	*gearbox*
14	Tourist Trophy–Aggregate	Oulton Park	01/05/65	Ian Walker-Team Lotus	Lotus 30-Ford	
1	Indianapolis 500	Indianapolis	31/05/65	Team Lotus	USAC Lotus 38-Ford 4-cam	
ret	Player's 200–Heat 1	Mosport Park	05/06/65	Ian Walker-Team Lotus	Lotus 30-Ford	*driveshaft*
1	London Trophy–Heat 1	Crystal Palace	07/06/65	Ron Harris-Team Lotus	F2 Lotus 35-Cosworth SCA	*Fastest lap*
1	London Trophy–Heat 2	Crystal Palace	07/06/65	Ron Harris-Team Lotus	F2 Lotus 35-Cosworth SCA	*Pole/Fastest lap*
1	London Trophy–Aggregate	Crystal Palace	07/06/65	Ron Harris-Team Lotus	F2 Lotus 35-Cosworth SCA	
1	**BELGIAN GP**	Spa	13/06/65	Team Lotus	F1 Lotus 33-Climax FWMV	*Fastest lap*

'And Graham says you ought to be paying me that much, but I'm not sure he's right…'

1965 (continued)

1	**FRENCH GP**	Clermont-Ferrand	27/06/65	Team Lotus	F1 Lotus 25-Climax FWMV	*Pole/Fastest lap*
3	Reims Grand Prix	Reims	03/07/65	Ron Harris-Team Lotus	F2 Lotus 35-Cosworth SCA	
1	**BRITISH GP**	Silverstone	10/07/65	Team Lotus	F1 Lotus 33-Climax FWMV	*Pole*
1	**DUTCH GP**	Zandvoort	18/07/65	Team Lotus	F1 Lotus 33-Climax FWMV	*Fastest lap*
1	**GERMAN GP**	Nürburgring	01/08/65	Team Lotus	F1 Lotus 33-Climax FWMV	*Pole/Fastest lap*
2	Mediterranean Grand Prix	Enna	15/08/65	Team Lotus	F1 Lotus 25-Climax FWMV	*Pole/Fastest lap*
Demo	Mountain climb	Ste Ursanne-Les Rangiers	22/08/65	Team Lotus	USAC Lotus 38-Ford 4-cam	
nc	Swiss Mountain Grand Prix	Ollon-Villars	29/08/65	Team Lotus	USAC Lotus 38-Ford 4-cam	*misfire*
1	British Eagle Trophy	Brands Hatch	30/08/65	Ron Harris-Team Lotus	F2 Lotus 35-Cosworth SCA	*Fastest lap*
10	Guards Trophy–Heat 1	Brands Hatch	30/08/65	Ian Walker-Team Lotus	Lotus 40-Ford	*2 spins*
ret	Guards Trophy–Heat 2	Brands Hatch	30/08/65	Ian Walker-Team Lotus	Lotus 40-Ford	*transmission*
nc	Guards Trophy–Aggregate	Brands Hatch	30/08/65	Ian Walker-Team Lotus	Lotus 40-Ford	
dsq	Saloon Cars unlimited	Brands Hatch	30/08/65	Team Lotus	Lotus-Cortina	*outside assistance/Fastest lap*
10/*ret*	**ITALIAN GP**	Monza	12/09/65	Team Lotus	F1 Lotus 33-Climax FWMV	*engine/Pole/Fastest lap*
6	Gold Cup	Oulton Park	18/09/65	Ron Harris-Team Lotus	F2 Lotus 35-Cosworth SCA	*spin/Fastest lap*
2	Saloon Cars unlimited	Oulton Park	18/09/65	Team Lotus	Lotus-Cortina	*1st in class/class Fastest lap*
ret	**US GP**	Watkins Glen	03/10/65	Team Lotus	F1 Lotus 33-Climax FWMV	*engine*
ret	**MEXICAN GP**	Mexico City	24/10/65	Team Lotus	F1 Lotus 33-Climax FWMV	*engine/Pole*
2	*Times* Grand Prix	Riverside	31/10/65	Ian Walker-Team Lotus	Lotus 40-Ford	

1966

ret	New Zealand Grand Prix	Pukekohe	08/01/66	Team Lotus	FT Lotus 39-Climax FPF	*gearbox*
2	Gold Leaf Trophy	Levin	15/01/66	Team Lotus	FT Lotus 39-Climax FPF	
2	Lady Wigram Trophy–Heat 1	Christchurch	22/01/66	Team Lotus	FT Lotus 39-Climax FPF	
ret	Lady Wigram Trophy–Final	Christchurch	22/01/66	Team Lotus	FT Lotus 39-Climax FPF	*collision with Gardner*
1=	Teretonga Trophy–Heat 2	Invercargill	29/01/66	Team Lotus	FT Lotus 39-Climax FPF	*dead heat with Stewart*
ret	Teretonga Trophy–Final	Invercargill	29/01/66	Team Lotus	FT Lotus 39-Climax FPF	*spun off*
1	Warwick Farm 100	Warwick Farm	13/02/66	Team Lotus	FT Lotus 39-Climax FPF	*Pole/Fastest lap*
2	Australian Grand Prix–Heat 2	Lakeside	20/02/66	Team Lotus	FT Lotus 39-Climax FPF	
3	Australian Grand Prix–Final	Lakeside	20/02/66	Team Lotus	FT Lotus 39-Climax FPF	
2	Sandown Park International–Preliminary	Sandown Park	26/02/66	Team Lotus	FT Lotus 39-Climax FPF	
2	Sandown Park International	Sandown Park	27/02/66	Team Lotus	FT Lotus 39-Climax FPF	
3	*Launceston Examiner* 45	Longford	05/03/66	Team Lotus	FT Lotus 39-Climax FPF	
7	South Pacific Trophy	Longford	06/03/66	Team Lotus	FT Lotus 39-Climax FPF	*pit stop–plugs*
dns	Spring Trophy	Oulton Park	03/04/66	Ron Harris-Team Lotus	F2 Lotus 35-Cosworth SCA	*race abandoned–weather/Pole*
dns	Saloon Cars–unlimited	Oulton Park	03/04/66	Team Lotus	Lotus-Cortina	*race abandoned–weather/Pole*
3	Saloon Cars–unlimited	Snetterton	08/04/66	Team Lotus	Lotus-Cortina	*1st in class/class Fastest lap*
ret	*Sunday Mirror* Trophy	Goodwood	11/04/66	Ron Harris-Team Lotus	F2 Lotus 35-Cosworth SCA	*puncture*
4	Saloon Cars unlimited	Goodwood	11/04/66	Team Lotus	Lotus-Cortina	*1st in class/class Fastest lap*
7	Pau Grand Prix	Pau	17/04/66	Ron Harris-Team Lotus	F2 Lotus 35-Cosworth SCA	*pit stop–battery*
ret	Juan Jover Trophy	Montjuich Park	24/04/66	Ron Harris-Team Lotus	F2 Lotus 44-Cosworth SCA	*engine*
ret	**MONACO GP**	Monte Carlo	22/05/66	Team Lotus	F1 Lotus 33-Climax FWMV	*suspension/Pole*
2	Indianapolis 500	Indianapolis	30/05/66	Granatelli STP-Team Lotus	USAC Lotus 38-Ford 4-cam	
ret	**BELGIAN GP**	Spa	13/06/66	Team Lotus	F1 Lotus 33-Climax FWMV	*spun off*
dns	**FRENCH GP**	Reims	03/07/66	Team Lotus	F1 Lotus 33-Climax FWMV	*hit in the face by bird*
4	**BRITISH GP**	Brands Hatch	16/07/66	Team Lotus	F1 Lotus 33-Climax FWMV	*pit stop–brakes*
3	**DUTCH GP**	Zandvoort	24/07/66	Team Lotus	F1 Lotus 33-Climax FWMV	*pit stops–water*
ret	**GERMAN GP**	Nürburgring	07/08/66	Team Lotus	F1 Lotus 33-Climax FWMV	*spun off/Pole*
3	Kanonloppet	Karlskoga	21/08/66	Ron Harris-Team Lotus	F2 Lotus 44-Cosworth SCA	
3	Suomen Grand Prix–Heat 1	Keimola	24/08/66	Ron Harris-Team Lotus	F2 Lotus 44-Cosworth SCA	
3	Suomen Grand Prix–Heat 2	Keimola	24/08/66	Ron Harris-Team Lotus	F2 Lotus 44-Cosworth SCA	
3	Suomen Grand Prix–Aggregate	Keimola	24/08/66	Ron Harris-Team Lotus	F2 Lotus 44-Cosworth SCA	
8	Guards Trophy–Heat 1	Brands Hatch	29/08/66	Felday Engineering	Felday 4-BRM 56	*1st in class/class Fastest lap*
dsq	Guards Trophy–Heat 2	Brands Hatch	29/08/66	Felday Engineering	Felday 4-BRM 56	*black-flagged–oil smoke*
nc	Guards Trophy–Aggregate	Brands Hatch	29/08/66	Felday Engineering	Felday 4-BRM 56	
1	Saloon Cars unlimited	Brands Hatch	29/08/66	Team Lotus	Lotus-Cortina	
ret	**ITALIAN GP**	Monza	04/09/66	Team Lotus	F1 Lotus 43-BRM 75	*wheel weights*
2	Grand Prix de l'Ile de France	Montlhéry	11/09/66	Ron Harris-Team Lotus	F2 Lotus 44-Cosworth SCA	*Fastest lap*
3	Gold Cup	Oulton Park	17/09/66	Team Lotus	F1 Lotus 33-Climax FWMV	
1	Saloon Cars unlimited	Oulton Park	17/09/66	Team Lotus	Lotus-Cortina	*class Fastest lap*
6	Trophée Craven 'A'	Le Mans	18/09/66	Ron Harris-Team Lotus	F2 Lotus 44-Cosworth SCA	*pit stop– throttle*
9	Albi Grand Prix	Albi	25/09/66	Ron Harris-Team Lotus	F2 Lotus 44-Cosworth SCA	*pit stop–fuel vaporisation*
1	**US GP**	Watkins Glen	02/10/66	Team Lotus	F1 Lotus 43-BRM 75	
dns	Indianapolis Cars	Mount Fuji	09/10/66	Granatelli STP-Team Lotus	USAC Lotus 38-Ford 4-cam	*engine*
ret	**MEXICAN GP**	Mexico City	23/10/66	Team Lotus	F1 Lotus 43-BRM 75	*throttle linkage*
3	Motor Show 200–Heat 1	Brands Hatch	30/10/66	Ron Harris-Team Lotus	F2 Lotus 44-Cosworth SCA	
3	Motor Show 200–Final	Brands Hatch	30/10/66	Ron Harris-Team Lotus	F2 Lotus 44-Cosworth SCA	
1	Saloon Cars unlimited–Heat 1	Brands Hatch	30/10/66	Team Lotus	Lotus-Cortina	*Pole/class Fastest lap*
15	Saloon Cars unlimited–Heat 2	Brands Hatch	30/10/66	Team Lotus	Lotus-Cortina	*pit stop–tyre*
10	Saloon Cars unlimited–Aggregate	Brands Hatch	30/10/66	Team Lotus	Lotus-Cortina	*3rd in class*
ret	RAC Rally	Great Britain	19–23/11/66	Ford Competition Department	Lotus-Cortina	*accident*

1967

ret	**SOUTH AFRICAN GP**	Kyalami	02/01/67	Team Lotus	F1 Lotus 43-BRM 75	*fuel system*
2	New Zealand Grand Prix	Pukekohe	07/01/67	Team Lotus	FT Lotus 33-Climax FWMV	*Fastest lap*
1	Wills Lovin International	Levin	14/01/67	Team Lotus	FT Lotus 33-Climax FWMV	*Pole/Fastest lap*
1	Lady Wigram Trophy	Christchurch	21/01/67	Team Lotus	FT Lotus 33-Climax FWMV	
1	Teretonga International	Invercargill	28/01/67	Team Lotus	FT Lotus 33-Climax FWMV	*Pole/Fastest lap*
1	Lakeside International	Lakeside	12/02/67	Team Lotus	FT Lotus 33-Climax FWMV	*Pole/Fastest lap*
2	Australian Grand Prix	Warwick Farm	19/02/67	Team Lotus	FT Lotus 33-Climax FWMV	
1	Sandown Park International	Sandown Park	26/02/67	Team Lotus	FT Lotus 33-Climax FWMV	
2	South Pacific Trophy–Heat 1	Longford	04/03/67	Team Lotus	FT Lotus 33-Climax FWMV	
3	South Pacific Trophy–Heat 2	Longford	04/03/67	Team Lotus	FT Lotus 33-Climax FWMV	
2	South Pacific Trophy–Final	Longford	06/03/67	Team Lotus	FT Lotus 33-Climax FWMV	
4	Pau Grand Prix	Pau	02/04/67	Team Lotus	F2 Lotus 48-Cosworth FVA	*pit stops/Pole/Fastest lap*
1	Juan Jover Trophy	Montjuich Park	09/04/67	Team Lotus	F2 Lotus 48-Cosworth FVA	*Fastest lap*
ret	Eifelrennen	Nürburgring	23/04/67	Team Lotus	F2 Lotus 48-Cosworth FVA	*gearbox/Pole*
ret	**MONACO GP**	Monte Carlo	07/05/67	Team Lotus	F1 Lotus 33-Climax FWMV	*suspension/crash/Fastest lap*
1	Limbourg Grand Prix–Heat 1	Zolder	21/05/67	Team Lotus	F2 Lotus 48-Cosworth FVA	*Fastest lap*
4	Limbourg Grand Prix–Heat 2	Zolder	21/05/67	Team Lotus	F2 Lotus 48-Cosworth FVA	*high water temp./Pole*
2	Limbourg Grand Prix–Aggregate	Zolder	21/05/67	Team Lotus	F2 Lotus 48-Cosworth FVA	
31/ret	Indianapolis 500	Indianapolis	30–31/05/67	Granatelli STP-Team Lotus	USAC Lotus 38-Ford 4-cam	*engine*
1	**DUTCH GP**	Zandvoort	04/06/67	Team Lotus	F1 Lotus 49-Cosworth DFV	*Fastest lap*
6	**BELGIAN GP**	Spa	18/06/67	Team Lotus	F1 Lotus 49-Cosworth DFV	*pit stop–plugs/Pole*
ret	Reims Grand Prix	Reims	25/06/67	Team Lotus	F2 Lotus 48-Cosworth FVA	*gear selector*
ret	**FRENCH GP**	Le Mans	02/07/67	Team Lotus	F1 Lotus 49-Cosworth DFV	*final drive*
ret	Rouen Grand Prix	Rouen	09/07/67	Team Lotus	F2 Lotus 48-Cosworth FVA	*puncture–crash*
1	**BRITISH GP**	Silverstone	15/07/67	Team Lotus	F1 Lotus 49-Cosworth DFV	*Pole*
ret	Flugplatzrennen	Tulln Langenlebarn	16/07/67	Team Lotus	F2 Lotus 48-Cosworth FVA	*puncture/Fastest lap*
1	Madrid Grand Prix	Jarama	23/07/67	Team Lotus	F2 Lotus 48-Cosworth FVA	*Fastest lap*
ret	**GERMAN GP**	Nürburgring	06/08/67	Team Lotus	F1 Lotus 49-Cosworth DFV	*suspension/Pole*
3	Swedish Grand Prix	Karlskoga	13/08/67	Team Lotus	F2 Lotus 48-Cosworth FVA	
7/ret	Mediterranean Grand Prix–Heat 1	Enna	20/08/67	Team Lotus	F2 Lotus 48-Cosworth FVA	*engine*
dns	Mediterranean Grand Prix–Heat 2	Enna	20/08/67	Team Lotus	F2 Lotus 48-Cosworth FVA	*engine*
nc	Mediterranean Grand Prix–Aggregate	Enna	20/08/67	Team Lotus	F2 Lotus 48-Cosworth FVA	
ret	**CANADIAN GP**	Mosport Park	27/08/67	Team Lotus	F1 Lotus 49-Cosworth DFV	*wet ignition/Pole*
1	Suomen Grand Prix–Preliminary Heat	Keimola	03/09/67	Team Lotus	F2 Lotus 48-Cosworth FVA	
1	Suomen Grand Prix–Final	Keimola	03/09/67	Team Lotus	F2 Lotus 48-Cosworth FVA	*Pole/Fastest lap*
3	Hämeenlinnan Ajot	Ahvenisto	05/09/67	Team Lotus	F2 Lotus 48-Cosworth FVA	*Pole*
3	**ITALIAN GP**	Monza	10/09/67	Team Lotus	F1 Lotus 49-Cosworth DFV	*pit stop–tyre/Pole/Fastest lap*
3	Albi Grand Prix	Albi	24/09/67	Team Lotus	F2 Lotus 44-Cosworth FVA	*spin*
1	**US GP**	Watkins Glen	01/10/67	Team Lotus	F1 Lotus 49-Cosworth DFV	
1	**MEXICAN GP**	Mexico City	22/10/67	Team Lotus	F1 Lotus 49-Cosworth DFV	*Pole/Fastest lap*
ret	American 500	Rockingham	29/10/67	Holman and Moody	Ford Fairlane	*engine*
1	Spanish Grand Prix	Jarama	12/11/67	Team Lotus	F1 Lotus 49-Cosworth DFV	*Pole/Fastest lap*
ret	Rex Mays 300	Riverside	26/11/67	Sperex Special Racing Team	USAC Vollstedt-Ford 4-cam	*engine*

1968

1	**SOUTH AFRICAN GP**	Kyalami	01/01/68	Team Lotus	F1 Lotus 49-Cosworth DFV	*Pole/Fastest lap*
ret	New Zealand Grand Prix	Pukekohe	08/01/68	Team Lotus	FT Lotus 49T-Cosworth DFW	*engine/Pole*
ret	Rothmans International	Levin	13/01/68	Team Lotus	FT Lotus 49T-Cosworth DFW	*damaged car–went off*
1	Lady Wigram Trophy	Christchurch	20/01/68	Gold Leaf Team Lotus	FT Lotus 49T-Cosworth DFW	*Pole/Fastest lap*
2	Teretonga Trophy	Invercargill	27/01/68	Gold Leaf Team Lotus	FT Lotus 49T-Cosworth DFW	*lost nose cone/Fastest lap*
1	Rothmans 100	Surfers Paradise	11/02/68	Gold Leaf Team Lotus	FT Lotus 49T-Cosworth DFW	
1	Warwick Farm 100	Warwick Farm	18/02/68	Gold Leaf Team Lotus	FT Lotus 49T-Cosworth DFW	*Pole*
1	Australian Grand Prix	Sandown Park	25/02/68	Gold Leaf Team Lotus	FT Lotus 49T-Cosworth DFW	
5	South Pacific Trophy	Longford	04/03/68	Gold Leaf Team Lotus	FT Lotus 49T-Cosworth DFW	
ret	Juan Jover Trophy	Montjuich Park	31/03/68	Gold Leaf Team Lotus	F2 Lotus 48-Cosworth FVA	*hit by Ickx*
ret	Deutschland Trophy–Heat 1	Hockenheim	07/04/68	Gold Leaf Team Lotus	F2 Lotus 48-Cosworth FVA	*fatal accident*

Formula 1 World Championship positions/points

1960	8th=	8	1965	1st	54
1961	7th=	11	1966	6th	16
1962	2nd	30	1967	3rd	41
1963	1st	73	1968	11th	9
1964	3rd	32			274

Formula 1 World Championship placings 1st–6th + Pole + Fastest lap

1st	2nd	3rd	4th	5th	6th	Pole	Fastest lap	Races
25	1	6	4	3	1	33	28	72

Note:

When Liz Le Breton told me that Doug Nye was writing this profile of Jim Clark, I was more than pleased. Then she mentioned that Doug thought that Clark could walk on water. What could I say except 'Well of course he could, couldn't he?' Nuff said.

*Shrimp Curve, Hockenheimring – no words exist for an
adequate epitaph…*